Literacy Strategies Across the Subject Areas

I0764722

Literacy Strategies Across the Subject Areas

Process-Oriented Blackline Masters for the K–12 Classroom

SECOND EDITION

Karen D. Wood
University of North Carolina at Charlotte

D. Bruce Taylor
University of North Carolina at Charlotte

PEARSON

Boston   New York   San Francisco
Mexico City   Montreal   Toronto   London   Madrid   Munich   Paris
Hong Kong   Singapore   Tokyo   Cape Town   Sydney

Senior Series Editor: *Aurora Martínez Ramos*
Series Editorial Assistant: *Kevin Shannon*
Senior Marketing Manager: *Krista Groshong*
Production Editor: *Janet Domingo*
Editorial-Production Service: *Omegatype Typography, Inc.*
Composition and Manufacturing Buyer: *Andrew Turso*
Electronic Composition: *Omegatype Typography, Inc.*
Cover Administrator: *Rebecca Krzyzaniak*

For related titles and support materials, visit our online catalog at www.ablongman.com.

Copyright © 2006, 2001 Pearson Education, Inc.

All rights reserved. No part of the material protected by this copyright notice may be reproduced or utilized in any form or by any means, electronic or mechanical, including photocopying, recording, or by any information storage and retrieval system, without written permission of the copyright owner.

To obtain permission(s) to use material from this work, please submit a written request to Allyn and Bacon, Permissions Department, 75 Arlington Street, Boston, MA 02116 or fax your request to 617-848-7320.

Between the time website information is gathered and then published, it is not unusual for some sites to have closed. Also, the transcription of URLs can result in typographical errors. The publisher would appreciate notification where these errors occur so that they may be corrected in subsequent editions.

ISBN 0-205-43712-5

Printed in the United States of America

10   9   8   7   6   5   4   3   2   1   10   09   08   07   06   05

Dedicated, as always, with love to my children:
Eric, Ryan, Lauren, and Kevin,
and to my husband, David.
—KDW

To Jon Maria, Nick, David, and Jake—my family—
who are with me in all things.
—DBT

Contents

Preface

We are pleased to introduce the second edition of *Literacy Strategies Across the Subject Areas*. This revision builds on the success of the first edition by providing teachers and their students with process-oriented blackline masters of literacy learning for use in kindergarten through grade 12. Most workbooks offer each student one set of problems. *Literacy Strategies Across the Subject Areas* offers teachers and students a flexible set of strategies that can help connect and support literacy learning within and across subject areas. Teachers model strategies that support learning in their content area and guide students toward independence in the use of those strategies.

Literacy Strategies Across the Subject Areas contains many of the features of the first edition. Each lesson includes:

- Title
- Objective
- Rationale/description
- Intended audience (grade and ability levels)
- Procedures
- Bibliographic information
- Sample lessons (where appropriate)
- Blackline master(s)

This edition contains several more strategies and offers examples from a wide array of subject areas including art, music, math, science, English language arts, and second language classes. Some strategies have been adapted for use with English language learners (ELL). The second edition recognizes that as technology becomes more pervasive and the use of computers, the Internet, and multimedia spread to the classroom and beyond, students and teachers need tools for gathering and evaluating web-based texts. Specific strategies such as the Web Page Evaluation Checklist (p. 16) are provided, and other strategies have been adapted for use with multimedia texts. The principles of this book are built on a strong base of research and theory.

Using Schema and Prior Knowledge in Constructing Meaning

Reading can be defined as the process of constructing meaning from text. It is a dynamic process that involves a continuous interaction between the reader and the text. It is most effective when readers are able to connect new information to prior knowledge. The importance of prior knowledge in comprehension and meaning making has been well-established in the professional literature (Anderson & Pearson, 1984; Tierney & Pearson, 1994). Our understanding of the significance of prior knowledge in literacy and reading has its roots in schema theory, the notion that individuals develop cognitive structures in their minds based on their varied experiences (Rumelhart, 1980). Students bring diverse knowledge and experiences into the classroom, and tapping into that allows students to connect new information and concepts with prior knowledge, thus improving comprehension. At the same time, there is a need to build a foundation of background knowledge to help students bridge the gap between new and familiar concepts. Several strategies included in this book seek to improve comprehension by drawing on this research-based understanding of learning. The KWL Plus and the IEPC strategies offer excellent opportunities for students and teachers to brainstorm together and make these important connections that foster comprehension.

An Effective Model of Instruction

Literacy learning and reading, in particular, are complex processes. A growing body of research affirms the importance of reading to subject-area learning. Research in science, mathematics, and social studies classes show many opportunities for listening, speaking, reading, and writing (Balas, 1997; Ediger, 2000; Fuentes, 1998). Research also points to problems between readers and texts in content-area classes and the need for support. Finley (1991) found that students lacked experience with the concepts and language of science classes. Freitag (1997) found a similar situation with regard to students' knowledge of the language of mathematical concepts, and argued that students need to learn to read mathematically. As Wells (1996) and others have suggested, students face struggles within schools and in moves across grade levels, and students who face difficulties often continue to do so (Irvin, Buehl, & Klemp, 2003).

Recent studies point to the potential for teaching strategies to support literacy learning and reading in content-area classrooms (Greenleaf, Schlenbach, Cziko, & Mueller, 2001). Rhoder (2002) states that strategy instruction is most effective when it is taught purposefully. She emphasizes the need for direct instruction and teacher modeling that leads to student mastery of strategies over time. She also cautions that teaching too many strategies in a short amount of time undermines transfer and student ownership.

Literacy Strategies Across the Subject Areas recognizes the dual roles of the teacher in teaching and modeling strategies for students who, in turn, practice and apply those skills and gain mastery over time. The phased transfer model of instruction (Wood, 2002), like most models of scaffolded instruction, places responsibility to introduce and model strategies with the teacher. The chart below lays out a sequence of instruction in which the teacher shares a strategy through thinking aloud and walking students through the procedures.

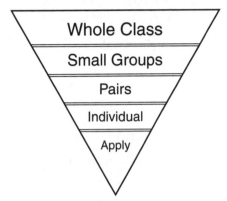

This is typically done in the form of whole class instruction, using content-specific texts and materials, while eliciting input from students. Small groups can provide a beneficial step toward student ownership and successful application of a strategy. Students can work with peers in practicing strategies and supporting others in learning while the teacher circulates and monitors, providing assistance where necessary. Next, the teacher may have students work in pairs for further practice and refinement of strategies before students implement strategies on their own. Many of the strategies presented in this book involve this phased transfer model of instruction. Students follow this sequence of whole class and small group instruction and independent practice with Story Maps and Frames (pp. 92–97). Two strategies that are new to this edition, Web Page Evaluation (pp. 11–17) and GIST (pp. 31–35), also follow this format.

Metacognition

Research has shown that metacognition—the awareness and monitoring of one's own thought processes, or "thinking about thinking"—aids students' understanding and recall (Baker & Brown, 1984; Brown, 1980). Strategies that support metacognition can help students become more self-reliant and strategic about their learning (Scheid, 1993).

Think alouds (Davey, 1983) are one of the ways in which teachers can help students become aware of their thought processes. In think alouds, teachers model or describe their thoughts about their reading of a text. This provides students with both a strategy and a glimpse at the cognitive process. For example, when a class comes across a challenging word or concept, rather than telling students a definition, the teacher can model a strategy for finding its meaning. Students learn both the word or concept and a strategy they can use in the future in similar situations.

Supporting Readers Throughout the Reading Process

Reading is a complex process that is thought to take place in stages. *Literacy Strategies Across the Subject Areas* seeks to support readers throughout the entire process and draws attention to three stages or places of support: prereading, reading, and postreading. The prereading stage is the time for explaining the purposes of texts and assignments, building students' background knowledge, introducing and preteaching significant vocabulary terms, making predictions, and helping students connect new information to what they already know. A strategy such as Story Impressions (pp. 98–101) aids teachers and students at this point in the reading process. The reading stage is the time for guiding students through the reading of the selection, helping them focus on the most significant information. The Personal Vocabulary Journal (pp. 19–24) supports readers during the reading process. The postreading stage is when students are asked to make sense of what they've read by returning to their original predictions and modifying them to coordinate with what was learned, as in the Probable Passage strategy (pp. 67–70). The postreading phase is time for synthesizing and discussing the new content, extending learning through writing or other assignments, as in List, Group, Label, and Write (pp. 6–10). Some strategies, such as KWL Plus (pp. 41–46), support reading across all three stages. A matrix (pp. xvii–xviii) is included that identifies these stages for each strategy included in this book.

Collaborative Learning

Collaborative learning holds potential to address many instructional needs of diverse learners (Tomlinson, 1999) and also helps connect classroom learning to a world in which we often work in collaboration with others. According to Johnson and Johnson (Brandt, 1987), there is more evidence for the benefits of collaborative learning than any other aspect of education. Research from many sources (Johnson & Johnson, 1991;

Kagan, 1994; Paratore & McCormack, 1997; Slavin, 1995) suggests that collaborative learning in the form of flexible grouping has been demonstrated to

- Improve peer relationships.
- Increase self-esteem and motivation.
- Aid students in accepting diversity.
- Improve achievement as measured on standardized tests.
- Improve performance across subject areas.
- Improve performance of ability levels.
- Decrease reliance on the teacher.

The second edition of *Literacy Strategies Across the Subject Areas* continues to foster the use of cooperative learning through student interaction in small groups and paired interaction. For example, students talk over their ideas about how to solve a problem or undertake a task in Think, Pair, Share (pp. 75–77). In Talking Drawings (pp. 1–5), students share their artistic interpretations of topics with a partner. Discussion Webs (pp. 83–86) offers students a chance to collaborate and come to a consensus on a topic.

Inquiry Learning

Inquiry is a student-centered approach to learning that involves asking questions and gathering information from a variety of sources in order to build new understandings. This approach to learning puts students at the center of research and problem solving and has often been associated with teaching and learning in science (e.g, see Saunders, 1992), although it has implications for learning in multiple subject areas. *Literacy Strategies Across the Subject Areas* offers a variety of strategies that support inquiry-based learning. The KWL Plus (pp. 41–46) can serve as a tool for guiding students' study of new concepts by building on what they know to what they want to know. Inquiry Charts (pp. 51–53), updated in this edition to include Internet-based information, provide a way for students to catalogue information they gain from multiple sources. The Web Page Evaluation Forms (pp. 11–18) help students evaluate and select the most appropriate texts obtained from the Internet.

Multiple Literacies

Literacy Strategies Across the Subject Areas also acknowledges that the definition of text has expanded. In the past, teachers and students may have relied primarily on print material such as textbooks and trade books. However, recent attention has been given to defining text more broadly to include a wide range of print materials, video, multimedia, hypertext, environmental print, classroom talk, and more. This edition of the book includes more diverse examples of texts, including hypertext and web pages from a broader range of content areas.

Meeting the Needs of Diverse Learners

Just as texts have become more diverse, so have the students in our classrooms. Some of the strategies in this book are targeted toward the needs of students who struggle. For example, Paired Reading for Fluency (pp. 64–66) is a repeated reading strategy that enables partners to practice reading short passages to build reading fluency. This strategy can also help students reading texts with difficult or archaic language. Acknowledging the wide range of texts and topics students encounter within and across grade levels, we believe that *all* students encounter literacy and reading challenges and thus benefit by having tools or strategies to deal with those challenges.

This book also points out where the needs of specific students can be addressed, particularly English language learners (ELL). In this edition we have added suggestions for modifying some strategies for use with language instruction, to build background knowledge and help students work from their primary language as a base for developing competencies in acquiring other languages. We have included suggestions for modifying the Personal Vocabulary Journal (pp. 19–24), Possible Sentences (pp. 54–59), and Paired Reading for Fluency (pp. 64–66).

It is our hope that *Literacy Strategies Across the Subject Areas* will be help teachers and students across all grade levels and subject areas (and those who support and work with them) adapt to an ever-changing world.

Acknowledgments

We would like to thank the following reviewers for their helpful comments on this edition: Mellinee Lesley, Texas Tech University; Linda K. Lilienthal, University of North Colorado; Dr. Mary Beth Marr, University of North Carolina at Charlotte; and Georgene Risko, Otterbein. A special thanks to teacher Chris Fisher for some of the sample lessons.

References

Anderson, R. C., & Pearson, P. D. (1984). A schema-theoretic view of basic processes in reading comprehension. In P. D. Pearson (Ed.), *Handbook of reading research* (pp. 255–291). New York: Longman.

Baker, L., & Brown, A. L. (1984). Metacognitive skills in reading. In P. D. Pearson (Ed.), *Handbook of reading research* (pp. 353–394). New York: Longman.

Balas, A. K. (1997). *The mathematics and reading connection.* ERIC Clearinghouse for Science, Mathematics, and Environmental Education. ERIC Document Reproduction Service No. ED432439.

Brandt, R. (1987). On cooperation in schools: A conversation with David and Roger Johnson. *Educational Leadership, 45*(3), 14–19.

Brown, A. L. (1980). Metacognitive development and reading. In R. J. Spiro, B. C. Bruce, & W. F. Brewer (Eds.), *Theoretical issues in reading comprehension* (pp. 453–481). Hillsdale, NJ: Lawrence Erlbaum.

Davey, B. (1983). Think-aloud—modeling the cognitive processes of reading comprehension. *Journal of Reading, 27*(1), pp. 44–47.

Ediger, M. (2000). *Language arts in the science curriculum.* ERIC Document Reproduction Service No. ED447492.

Finley, F. N. (1991). Why students have trouble learning from science texts. In C. M. Santa, & D. E. Alvermann (Eds.), *Science learning: Processes and applications.* Newark, DE: International Reading Association.

Freitag, M. (1997). Reading and writing in the mathematics classroom. *Mathematics Educator, 8* (1), 16–21.

Fuentes, P. (1998). Reading comprehension in mathematics. *Clearing House, 72*(2), 81–88.

Greenleaf, C. L., Schlenbach, R., Cziko, C., & Mueller, F. L. (2001). Apprenticing adolescent readers to academic literacy. *Harvard Educational Review, 71*(1), pp. 79–127.

Irvin, J. L., Buehl, D. R., & Klemp, R. M. (2003). *Reading and the high school student: Strategies to enhance literacy.* Boston: Allyn and Bacon.

Johnson, D. W., & Johnson, R. T. (1991). *Learning together and alone* (3rd ed.). Boston: Allyn and Bacon.

Kagan, S. (1994). *Cooperative learning.* San Juan, CA: Kagan Cooperative Learning.

Paratore, J. R., McCormack, R. L. (Eds.) (1997). *Peertalk in the classroom: Learning from Research.* Newark, DE: International Reading Association.

Rhoder, C. (2002). Mindful reading: Strategy training that facilitates transfer. *Journal of Adolescent & Adult Literacy, 45,* 498–512.

Rumelhart, D. E. (1980). Schemata: The building blocks of cognition. In R. J. Spiro (Ed.), *Theoretical issues in reading comprehension* (pp. 33–58). Hillsdale, NJ: Lawrence Erlbaum.

Saunders, W. L. (1992). The constructivist approach: Implications and teaching strategies for science. *School Science and Mathematics, 92*(3), 136–141.

Scheid, K. (1993). *Helping students become strategic learners: Guidelines for teaching.* Cambridge, MA: Brookline Books.

Slavin, R. (1995). *Cooperative learning* (2nd ed.). Boston: Allyn and Bacon.

Tierney, R. J., & Pearson, P. D. (1994). Learning to learn from text: A framework for improving classroom practice. In R. B. Ruddell, M. R. Ruddell, & H. Singer (Eds.), *Theoretical models and processes of reading* (4th ed., pp. 496–513). Newark, DE: International Reading Association.

Tomlinson, C. A. (1999). *The differentiated classroom: Responding to the needs of all learners.* Alexandria, VA: Association for Supervision and Curriculum Development.

Wells, M. C. (1996). *Literacies lost: When students move from a progressive middle school to a traditional school.* New York: Teachers College Press.

Wood, K. D. (2002). Differentiating reading and writing lessons to promote content learning. In C. C. Block, L. B. Gambrell, & M. Pressley (Eds.), *Improving comprehension* (pp. 155–180). San Francisco: Jossey Bass.

STRATEGY	FOCUS Comprehension (C), Vocabulary (V), Critical Thinking (CT)			READING STAGE (Prereading, During Reading, Postreading)		
	C	V	CT	Pre	During	Post
Talking Drawings	●			●		
List-Group-Label and Write	●	●		●		
Web Page Evaluation Forms			●		●	
Personal Vocabulary Journal		●			●	
Semantic Feature Analysis		●		●	●	
Language Charts	●					●
GIST	●				●	●
Anticipation Guide	●		●	●		
KWL Plus	●		●	●	●	●
Collaborative Listening–Viewing Guide (CLVG)	●			●	●	
Inquiry Charts (I-Charts)	●			●	●	●
Possible Sentences		●		●		●
Exchange Compare Writing		●		●		
Paired Reading for Fluency	●				●	
Probable Passages		●	●	●	●	●
Herringbone Technique		●			●	●
Think, Pair, Share			●	●		●
Double Entry Journal			●		●	●
Discussion Webs	●		●			●
Imagine, Elaborate, Predict, and Confirm (IEPC)	●			●	●	●
Story Maps and Frames	●					●

STRATEGY	FOCUS Comprehension (C), Vocabulary (V), Critical Thinking (CT)			READING STAGE (Prereading, During Reading, Postreading)		
	C	V	CT	Pre	During	Post
Story Impressions	●			●		
Paired Comprehension and Retelling	●			●		
RAFT			●			

STRATEGY 1

Talking Drawings

Objective: To promote the use of prior knowledge in the improvement of recall and comprehension

Rationale/Description: Creating mental images before and after reading a selection to help students connect what is known about a topic with what is to be newly learned is a proven way to enhance student understanding and recall. Talking Drawings is a strategy in which students draw pictures of their mental images of a topic, character, or event before reading a selection and talk about and analyze the drawings with partners. After reading the selection, each student constructs another drawing that depicts the newly learned knowledge.

Intended for: Elementary, intermediate, middle, and secondary students and students who need additional support

Procedures:

Prereading Stage

Step One: Ask students to close their eyes and imagine the topic, event, or character to be studied. Then tell them to open their eyes and draw what they saw in their minds.

Step Two: Have the students share their drawings with at least two other students. Here they can talk about and analyze why they depicted the topic as they did.

Step Three: Then the students can share their thinking and drawings with the whole class, explaining personal experiences and sources of information that helped them in their drawings. From the whole class discussion, a concept map or cluster of information can be written on the board, reflecting the contributions of the class.

Reading Stage

Step Four: Have the students open their textbooks to the appropriate selection or distribute the relevant reading material and have them read the passage with their drawings in mind.

Postreading Stage

Step Five: Engage in a small group or whole class discussion of the selection and then ask the students to develop a new drawing or change the existing one to correspond with the new information.

Step Six: Have the students share and compare their before and after drawings with partners or group members, discussing the reasons for the changes made. Students can be encouraged to return to the selection to read aloud specific parts in the passage that support the changes they made.

Step Seven (Optional): Have the students write what they have changed from drawing one to drawing two.

Step Eight: The new learning can be extended by having the students further research related areas of the topic on the Internet or through other available sources.

Source: Based on McConnell, S. (1992/3). Talking drawings: A strategy for assisting learners. *Journal of Reading, 36*(4), 260–269.

Talking Drawings Sample Exercise—Narrative

1. Close your eyes and think about **a wolf.** Now open your eyes and draw what you saw.

2. Read/listen to *Wolf* **by Becky Bloom,** then draw a second picture to show what you learned.

3. In the space below, tell how your before picture is different from your after picture.

   The wolf in this story isn't like the one in Little Red Riding Hood. He starts off mean and tries to scare everyone. Then, he watches the cow, pig and duck love to read. He wants to impress his friends. So, he decides he better learn to read, too.

Talking Drawings Sample Exercise—Expository

1. Close your eyes and think about **volcanoes.** Now open your eyes and draw what you saw.

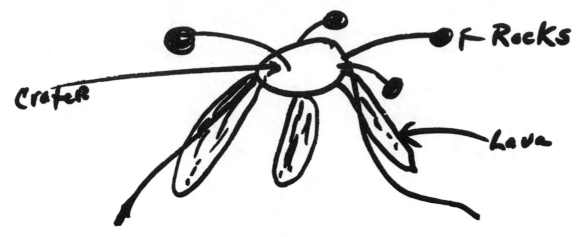

2. Read **your selection on volcanoes from Chapter 12,** then draw a second picture to show what you learned.

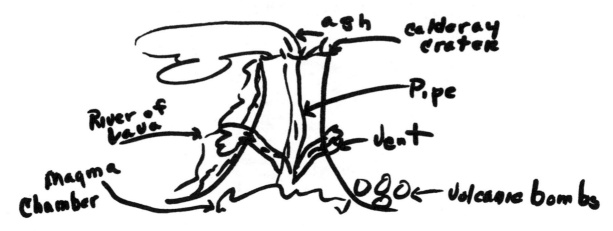

3. In the space below, tell what you have changed about your before and after pictures.

At first, I only drew the mountain and the lava coming down the sides. From our textbook and the video, I learned that there is a magma chamber inside that causes the eruption to flow throw the pipe and out the caldera, the huge opening at the top. There is a river of lava that flows down the side of the mountain. Ash and volcanic bombs can be seen around the volcano.

Talking Drawings Form

1. Close your eyes and think about _____. Now open your eyes and draw what you saw.

2. Read _____, then draw a second picture to show what you learned.

3. In the space below, tell what you have changed about your before and after pictures.

   _____

   _____

   _____

   _____

   _____

STRATEGY 2

List, Group, Label, and Write

Objective: To help students use their prior knowledge to improve their vocabulary, comprehension, and writing

Rationale/Description: The ability to group and class terms or concepts on the basis of their common elements is a higher order thinking skill. List, Group, Label, and Write is a brainstorming strategy in which students recall as many terms as possible on a given topic and then group these terms according to their similarities. It can be used before and after reading a selection.

Intended for: Elementary, intermediate, middle, and secondary students

Procedures:

Prereading Stage

> **Step One:** Tell the class to think of all the words that come to their minds on the topic to be studied. The topic could be anything about which they have some prior knowledge. Then display these terms on the board or an overhead transparency. The teacher may chose to introduce (preteach) significant terms at this time as well.

> **Step Two:** Either as a class or in small, heterogeneous groups, have students group the terms displayed. They may need to explain why they choose to put certain words/phrases in a particular category.

Reading Stage

> **Step Three:** After engaging the class in any other background building activities related to the topic (e.g., watching a brief video clip, viewing pictures, demonstrations, reading a picture storybook), have the students read the selection.

Postreading Stage

> **Step Four:** Tell the students to brainstorm about what they have learned on the topic after reading the selection. Display these associations as in Step One. (Some of the terms mentioned previously may be repeated to validate what they knew before reading.)

> **Step Five:** Again, have the students group and classify the terms displayed, justifying the categories if needed.

Step Six: Ask students to work individually or in pairs or to choose a group of terms about which to write a brief paragraph. Students should look at the categories or groups they developed in Step Two. It may be necessary to model the composition of one of more paragraphs with the entire class before releasing the responsibility to the students. They can be encouraged to use the terms displayed and to refer to the selection whenever necessary.

Source: Based on Taba, H. (1967). *Teachers' handbook for elementary social studies.* Adapted by Wood, K. D. (1986). Smuggling writing into middle level classrooms. *Middle School Journal.*

List, Group, Label, and Write Sample Exercise—Mathematics

Topic: Geometry

Step 1: **Free associations** (by whole class)

point	circumference	obtuse
line	semicircle	radius
diameter	center	compass
arc	vertex	ray
protractor	pi	sides
acute	right	endpoint
chord		ratio
line segment		

Step 2: **Grouping and labeling** (by students as a class, in pairs, or in small groups)

Terms about angles: vertex, sides, ray, endpoint

Devices for measurement: compass, protractor

Terms about circles: chord, arc, circumference, diameter, semicircle, radius, center, pi

Types of angles: acute, right, obtuse

Used in formula for pi: circumference, diameter, ratio

Units of length: point, line, endpoint, ray, line segment

Step 3: **Sample writing exercise** (by students in groups or pairs)

Angles are figures formed by two rays that have the same endpoints. The endpoint is called the vertex. The rays are called the sides of the angle.

Source: Adapted from Wood, K. D. (1986). How to "smuggle" writing into classrooms. *Middle School Journal,* 18(3), 5–6. Adapted from Taba, H. (1967). *Teachers' handbook for elementary social studies.* Reading, MA: Addison Wesley. Reprinted with permission from Karen Wood and the National Middle School Association.

List, Group, Label, and Write Sample Exercise

1. BEFORE READING: With your partner(s), list all of the terms that come to your mind on the topic volcanoes.

lava	Vesuvius	Hawaii	heat
hot	erupt	active-erupt	Mt. St. Helen
magma	dormant	caldera (opening)	extinct
ashes	mountain	Mexico	Krakatoa

2. Now, with the aid of your group members, group and label the terms.

Places	Names	Types	Parts
Mexico	Mt. St. Helen	dormant	caldera
Hawaii	Krakatoa	active-erupt	ashes
mountain	Vesuvius	extinct	lava

3. Share your grouped terms with the whole class.

4. Read your assigned selection.

5. AFTER READING: With the aid of your partner, write down as many new terms as you can. Talk about what you have learned.

intermittent	volcanic bombs	Japan	magma chamber
gas	rock fragments	Italy	rock
melt	ten miles	cinders	baseball

6. Group and label these new terms.

Beginning	Volcanic materials	Stages	Places
magma	lava	dormant	Hawaii
rock	rock fragments	active	Italy
melt	gas	extinct	Mexico
magma chamber	basketball	intermittent	Japan
ten miles			

7. Choose a grouping from the above list to write about on the lines below.

There are three types of volcanic materials that erupt from a volcano. Lava is magma that comes out and blows down. Rock fragments can be large or small. Some are as big as basketballs. Gas or steam also comes out of the caldera.

List, Group, Label, and Write

1. BEFORE READING: With your partner(s), list all of the terms that come to your mind on the topic of _____.

2. Now, with the aid of your group members, group and label the terms.

3. Read the assigned selection.

4. AFTER READING: With the aid of your partner(s), write down as many new terms as you can.

5. Group and label these new terms.

6. Choose a grouping from the above list to write about on the lines below.

   _____

   _____

   _____

   _____

   _____

  Copyright © 2006 Allyn and Bacon, Pearson Education, Inc.

STRATEGY 3

Web Page Evaluation

Objective: To help students evaluate information they obtain from the Internet

Rationale/Description: Many students use the Internet as a tool for finding information for both school assignments and personal interest. Evaluation forms including the Web Page Evaluation Checklist provide teachers and students with a tool for evaluating and thinking critically about the content of these texts.

Intended for: Elementary, intermediate, middle, and secondary students who are researching information on the Internet

Procedures:

Modeling/Demonstration Phase

Step One: The teacher or students decide on a topic to investigate or research.

Step Two: The teacher displays the Web Page Evaluation Checklist on an overhead projector and explains to the students that they will use the checklist to compare and evaluate Internet sources.

Step Three: Use a sample topic and websites to demonstrate the use of the checklist. Review questions with students and think aloud with students about the websites.

Guided Practice Phase

Step Four: The teacher monitors students in a computer lab or other place where the students can begin their online research. The teacher moves around the room and answers students' questions and helps individuals or groups as they evaluate Internet sources.

Step Five: Have students share some of their experiences and decisions as a whole class.

Application Phase

Step Six: Have students use the Web Page Evaluation Checklist as they conduct Internet-based research. Students can turn in the checklist with research results.

Source: Based on Barker, J. (2004). *The best stuff on the web.* Berkeley: The Teaching Library, University of California; Burke, J. (2000). *Reading reminders: Tools, tips, and techniques.* Portsmouth, NH: Boynton/Cook Publishers; Nielson, J. (2001). The three C's of critical web use: Collect, compare, and choose. *Useit.com Alertbox.* Retrieved from http://www.useit.com/alertbox/20010415.html

---

Web Page Evaluation Checklist Sample Exercise

REMEMBER: Think critically about every page you find.

	Title of page you are evaluating: World Factbook—Turkey	Title of page you are evaluating: Turkey General Information
1. Look at the URL:		
Personal page or site?	U.S. Government site	Travel Site
What type of domain is it? Is it appropriate for the content?	___ .com ___ .org/.net ___ .edu **X** .gov/mil/us ___ non-U.S.: _____ ___ other: _____	**X** .com ___ .org/.net ___ .edu ___ .gov/mil/us ___ non-U.S.: _____ ___ other: _____
Who is the publisher? Does the publisher make sense? Does it correspond to the name of the site?	Publisher or Domain Name: U.S. Central Intelligence Agency (CIA)—makes sense	Publisher or Domain Name: Turkey-eztravel.com—makes sense
2. Scan the page, looking for answers to these questions:		
Who wrote the page?	___ E-mail: ___ Name: CIA staff	___ E-mail: ___ Name: no author listed
Is there a date? **Is it current or old?**	Date: May 2004 Current enough? Yes	Date: _____ Current enough? _____
Credentials on this subject?	Evidence?	Evidence?
3. Look for these indicators of quality:		
Are sources well documented?	Good documentation	Little documentation on sources
Is the information complete? Is it altered or made up?	Seems complete, thorough	General information with less detail. No negative information.

Are there links to other sources? Do they work?	Links to other Factbook sources, not other sites	Links to hotels, car rental, tourism sites
Are other viewpoints included? Is the information biased?	Mostly information, facts	Seems like only positive information and viewpoints

4. What do others say about the site?

Who links to this site? Check search engines.	Many or few? **Many links** Opinions of it? **Seem favorable**	Many or few? **Some** Opinions of it? **No negative opinions found**
Is this page rated in a directory? http://about.com	Yes	No
Look up the author on a search engine.	N/A	N/A

5. Does it all add up?

Why was this page put out on the Web?	**X** Inform (facts, data) ___ Explain ___ Persuade ___ Sell ___ Entice ___ Share ___ Other: _____	**X** Inform (facts, data) ___ Explain ___ Persuade **X** Sell **X** Entice ___ Share ___ Other: _____
Possibly ironic? Satire or parody?	No	No
Is the information as good as other sources?	Seems like a good source. Includes positive and negative information	Okay for basic facts but does not provide any negative information

The Three Cs of Web Use: Collect, Compare, Choose
Sample Exercise—Fourth Grade Unit on Dinosaurs

Names of group members: <u>David, Kelley, Mandee, Terrell</u>

	Website:	Website:	Website:
COLLECT	www.dinosauria.com	pubs.usgs.gov/gip/dinosaurs	search.eb.com/dinosaurs
COMPARE **(Strengths and weaknesses)**	• Lots of information about dinosaurs collected by one person • Some of it is harder to read (very scientific) • Some good photos and pictures	• Government website • Answers questions about dinosaurs • Not as much information but easy to read • No photos	• Encyclopedia website • A lot of information • Easy to read and easy to find • Good charts and pictures
CHOOSE **(Which site will best help me?)**	This website is harder to read and find information. Seems like a good source for older students. **Not the best site for us to use.**	Answers questions that we want to know. Is a good source but does not have all the information we need and it does not have pictures. **A good choice for us to use.**	Good overall website. Has lots of information but it is easy to find and use. Good pictures and timelines. **A great choice for us to use.**

The Three Cs of Web Use: Collect, Compare, Choose

Names of group members: _____

	Website:	Website:	Website:
COLLECT			
COMPARE **(Strengths and weaknesses)**			
CHOOSE **(Which site will best help me?)**			

Copyright © 2006 Allyn and Bacon, Pearson Education, Inc.

Web Page Evaluation Checklist

REMEMBER: Think critically about every page you find.

	Title of page you are evaluating:	Title of page you are evaluating:
1. Look at the URL:		
Personal page or site?		
What type of domain is it? Is it appropriate for the content?	___ .com ___ .org/.net ___ .edu ___ .gov/mil/us ___ non-U.S.: _____ ___ other: _____	___ .com ___ .org/.net ___ .edu ___ .gov/mil/us ___ non-U.S.: _____ ___ other: _____
Who is the publisher? Does the publisher make sense? Does it correspond to the name of the site?	Publisher or Domain Name:	Publisher or Domain Name:
2. Scan the page, looking for answers to these questions:		
Who wrote the page?	___ E-mail: ___ Name:	___ E-mail: ___ Name:
Is there a date? Is it current or old?	Date: Current enough?	Date: Current enough?
Credentials on this subject?	Evidence?	Evidence?
3. Look for these indicators of quality:		
Are sources well documented?		
Is the information complete? Is it altered or made up?		
Are there links to other sources? Do they work?		

Copyright © 2006 Allyn and Bacon, Pearson Education, Inc.

Are other viewpoints included? Is the information biased?		

4. What do others say about the site?

Who links to this site? Check search engines.	Many or few? Opinions of it?	Many or few? Opinions of it?
Is this page rated in a directory? http://about.com		
Look up the author on a search engine.		

5. Does it all add up?

Why was this page put out on the Web?	___ Inform (facts, data) ___ Explain ___ Persuade ___ Sell ___ Entice ___ Share ___ Other: _____	___ Inform (facts, data) ___ Explain ___ Persuade ___ Sell ___ Entice ___ Share ___ Other: _____
Possibly ironic? Satire or parody?		
Is the information as good as other sources?		

Copyright © 2006 Allyn and Bacon, Pearson Education, Inc.

Web Page Information—Evaluation

INFORMATION

Thinking about the site:

- Who is responsible for the information on the website?
- When was the site last updated?
- When was the information on the site written?
- Does the information seem current or out of date?
- Has it won any awards? (Is there a link that gives information about the award?)

Thinking about the author of the site:

- Who is the author of the information on this site?
- What information can you find out about the author?
- Does the author seem to have the authority or knowledge to write about this topic?
- Does the site provide a section with information on the author or organization that published the site?

Thinking about the audience for the site:

- Does the site seem to have a specific audience?
- Does the site have advertisements? If so, what kind?
- If there are advertisements, do they tell you something about the intended audience for the site?

Thinking about information found on the site:

- Has the information been published someplace other than the Internet?
- Is the information clear and easy to understand?
- If the information is controversial, is more than point of view presented?
- Can you tell what information on the site is factual and what is opinion?
- Is quoted information clearly identified and properly cited?

EVALUATION

Overall, this site:

____ Would help me a lot with my assignment
____ Links me to other sites that are helpful
____ Looks helpful but the information is too technical or hard to understand
____ Is more an advertisement than information I can use
____ Seems to be just one person's or group's opinion or may not be reliable

Copyright © 2006 Allyn and Bacon, Pearson Education, Inc.

STRATEGY 4

Personal Vocabulary Journal

Objective: To enable students to select their own vocabulary words to develop and increase their vocabulary knowledge

Rationale/Description: Most vocabulary words learned by students are determined by the teacher, usually through commercially prepared materials and textbooks. Consequently, students do not have the opportunity to learn vocabulary words of their own choosing, based on their individual interests. The Personal Vocabulary Journal can be used by teachers at all grade levels and subject areas to help focus students' attention on new words of interest throughout their daily life at home or at school.

Intended for: Students of all grade levels, ability levels, and subject areas

Procedures:

Step One: Ask if the students if they have ever heard or read a word in or out of class and wondered what it meant. Also, ask if they would like to have the opportunity to choose their own words to study instead of having the teacher decide which are most important.

Step Two: Display a blank vocabulary form on an overhead projector or in a handout. Tell the students that they will use this form to record one or two (or more) vocabulary terms that interest them or that relate to the particular unit of study.

Step Three: Demonstrate a sample entry by thinking aloud the process students would undergo to select and record their entries. Enlist the participation of the class whenever possible.

Step Four: Make copies of the Personal Vocabulary Journal master and distribute to the class. Explain that they may be asked to keep a vocabulary journal for other subjects as well. Also explain that they may be asked to choose any word encountered that interests them, not necessarily one that is related to a topic studied in class.

Step Five (Discussion option): Students can be assigned to small groups of five to eight students to share words from their vocabulary journals. When appropriate, they may be asked to act out their words or make drawings to depict their meanings.

Step Six (Assessment option): Students may be asked to select two or three words from their Personal Vocabulary journals for the weekly or unit vocabulary test. These terms can be submitted to the teacher for assessment purposes.

> **ELL TIP:** ■ *The Personal Vocabulary Journal can be adapted for use with English language learners and second language learners. Have students write vocabulary words in both languages. They can include definitions and examples in both languages.*

Source: Based on Wood, K. D. (1994). *Practical strategies for improving instruction.* Columbus, OH: National Middle School Association.

Personal Vocabulary Journal Sample Exercise

My new word is squall

It is related to our science unit on weather

I found it on the weather station on TV

The specific context is New Yorkers were surprised with a thick squall early this morning.
No precipitation is expected tomorrow, however.

I think it means rain storm

The appropriate dictionary definition is a sudden gust of wind; a black squall has dark
clouds; a thick squall has hail or sleet

It reminds me of the word "squall" used in our Language Arts story which meant
"to scream."

My sentence is: The black squall scared the young children as they played ball in
the street.

Personal Vocabulary Journal
Sample Exercise—English Language Learners

	Spanish	English
My new word is	esfera	sphere
It is related to	geometria	geometry
I found it	en el libro de texto	the textbook
I think it means	bola o pelota	a ball
Definition	un objecto esferico o una pelota	spherical object or ball
Example	Un baloncesto es una esfersa.	A basketball is a sphere.
Picture		

Personal Vocabulary Journal

My new word is		
It is related to		
I found it		
I think it means		
Definition		
Example		
Picture		

Copyright © 2006 Allyn and Bacon, Pearson Education, Inc.

Personal Vocabulary Collection

My new word is _____

It is related to _____

I found it _____

The specific context is _____

_____

_____

_____

I think it means _____

The appropriate dictionary definition is _____

_____

_____

It reminds me of _____

_____

_____

My sentence is _____

_____

_____

_____

_____

  Copyright © 2006 Allyn and Bacon, Pearson Education, Inc.

STRATEGY 5

Semantic Feature Analysis

Objective: To help fine tune students' understanding of key vocabulary and concepts

Rationale/Description: This strategy uses a matrix to help students see the common elements and differences among key concepts being studied. Questioning and writing can be used to further solidify their understanding of the key terms.

Intended for: Elementary, intermediate, middle, and secondary students

Procedures:

Step One: Select a category based on a topic being studied in which at least two items are similar. For example, choose animals, elements, planets, explorers, scientific classes, words with similar meanings, historical or literary characters, and so on.

Step Two: Write or type the features of the category chosen across the top of the matrix provided.

Step Three: Write or type the terms or concepts on the left-hand side of the matrix.

Step Four: Make an overhead transparency of the matrix and display it on an overhead projector. Explain to the students that examining the terms this way will help them further understand the concepts.

Step Five: Model one or two examples as a class to explicate the process. Then guide the students through the matrix as a whole class, in groups or pairs, or individually by having them indicate with a plus (+) if an item contains a certain feature or a minus (–) if it does not.

Step Six: Help the students make some generalizations about the concepts by guiding them with specific questions. For example, "How is _____ different from or similar to _____?" or "Which is the longest (hottest, smallest, etc.)?"

Step Seven (Optional): Have students write down some key concepts they have learned from using in this strategy.

Source: Based on Johnson, D. D., & Pearson, P. D. (1984). *Teaching reading vocabulary* (2nd ed.). New York: Holt, Rinehart, and Winston.

Semantic Feature Analysis
Sample Exercise—Geography/Economics

Category: Products of the Thirteen Colonies

	Grain	Tobacco	Iron	Cattle	Furs	Lumber	Naval supplies
Connecticut	–	–	+	+	–	–	–
Massachusetts	+	–	+	+	–	–	+
New Hampshire	–	–	–	–	+	–	+
Rhode Island	–	–	+	–	–	–	–
Delaware	–	+	–	–	–	–	–
Maryland	–	+	–	+	–	–	–
New Jersey	–	–	+	–	–	–	–
New York	+	–	+	+	+	+	–
Pennsylvania	+	–	+	+	+	+	–
Georgia	–	–	–	–	+	–	–
North Carolina	+	+	–	+	+	+	+
South Carolina	+	–	–	–	–	+	+
Virginia	+	+	–	–	+	–	–

Summary

What conclusions can you draw by studying the information on the chart?

These thirteen colonies produced many types of goods. Furs were gathered in states from

north to south, but cattle were more common in the north than the south. Naval supplies were

made only in states near the coast, and tobacco was grown mostly in the middle states.

Semantic Feature Analysis Form

Summary

What conclusions can you draw by studying the information on the chart?

_____

_____

_____

STRATEGY 6

Language Charts

Objective: To help students better comprehend and retain information about literary texts

Rationale/Description: A language chart enables students to save and recall their ideas about literature selections they have read (usually on related topics or themes). With the help of the teacher, students use the chart to recall other stories in a unit and to notice similarities and differences. The language chart is most effective when comparing two or more books that share some common element (such as theme, topic, genre, author, illustrator), although it can be used after the reading of a single selection to help students recap the events and story line.

Intended for: Elementary, intermediate, middle, and secondary students

Procedures:

Step One: The teacher may choose to use the blank language chart included here or the chart can be drawn on a large piece of butcher paper. Present the blank form on an overhead projector and explain its purpose as a means of organizing ideas about literature selections.

Step Two: In the left column, write in the titles and authors of the selections being studied. Along the top of the chart, the teacher may also write in the questions to be considered or elicit questions from the students.

Step Three: Students and teacher share their thinking about the questions posed and how the responses are similar or different for each story read. These responses are recorded in the appropriate places on the language chart.

Options:

- The language charts for each theme being studied can be enlarged, decorated with student's artwork and comments, and displayed in the classroom.
- Students can work as a whole class or they can be divided into groups to fill in information on group copies of the language chart.
- Teachers can use response journals in combination with language charts by asking students to take a few minutes immediately after reading a story to record their personal reflections. (For emergent readers these may take the form of illustrations, whereas for more experienced readers and writers the responses may be more extensive.) Then the teachers can ask students to volunteer their responses each day as a stimulus for group discussion. Finally, after a thorough exploration of their thinking and talking, the collective responses are recorded on the language chart.

Source: Based on Roser, N. L., Hoffman, J. V., Labbo, L. D., & Farest, C. (1992) Language charts: A record of story time talk. *Language Arts, 69,* 44–52.

Language Chart Sample Exercise

Title, author	Characters	Main problem(s), issue(s), event(s)	How did their relationship change?	What was learned?
The Cay Theodore Taylor (Adventure)	Phillip, 11 years old, is shipwrecked with Timothy, a West Indian	Phillip doesn't trust Timothy at first and isn't nice to him.	Timothy helps Phillip when he goes blind.	That we are all human beings and deserve respect.
Crash Jerry Spinelli (Sports)	Crash Coogan, a 7th grade football star; Mike, his friend and a prankster; Webb, a nerd who is picked on	(1) Crash's grandfather has a stroke. (2) Mike and Crash pick on Webb for being different.	Webb gives Crash a present to help cure his sick grandfather and Crash helps Webb win the race.	That people who are different can be great friends.
Shiloh Phyllis Reynolds Naylor	Marty Preston, an 11 year-old; Shiloh, a dog nobody wants; Judd, the dog's mean owner	Marty finds a mistreated beagle pup and hides it in the woods, away from his parents.	Marty offers to work for Judd so that he may keep the dog; he also agrees to keep quiet about Judd's deer hunting.	That lying only leads to more problems, but it is important to help animals and people.
To Kill a Mockingbird Harper Lee	Scout and Jem Finch; their father Atticus Finch; Tom Robinson, a black man accused of rape; Boo Radley, a neighbor who never comes out of his house	Atticus is a lawyer who agrees to defend Tom Robinson, who is wrongly accused of rape. Many in the community are angry with Atticus for defending Tom. Boo saves the children from being attacked.	Scout and Jem learn to respect their father for his moral stand. They also learn that not all people are as they seem—Boo Radley for example. They grow up in the novel.	Scout and Jem learn about the evils of racism and come to understand that people can be good and evil.
Romeo and Juliet William Shakespeare	Romeo Montague, and Lady Montague; Benvolio and Mercutio, Romeo's friends; Juliet Capulet; and Lady Capulet; Tybalt, Juliet's hot-headed cousin; Friar Lawrence; the Prince, ruler of Verona and Paris	Romeo and Juliet, whose families are in a bitter feud, fall in love. They marry in secret but things fall apart when Romeo kills Juliet's cousin, Tybalt. Friar Lawrence tries to save them but they die in each other's arms when the plan fails.	The families are nearly destroyed by the violence of the feud.	That hatred can have terrible consequences.

Language Chart Form

Title, author			

Copyright © 2006 Allyn and Bacon, Pearson Education, Inc.

STRATEGY 7

GIST

Objective: To help students with comprehension by having them create condensed summaries of text selections

Rationale/Description: GIST stands for Generating Interactions between Schemata and Text. This strategy fosters comprehension by having students condense or summarize longer texts, allowing students to put concepts into their own words. GIST works especially well with expository and content-area texts.

Intended for: Elementary, middle, and secondary students

Procedures:

Modeling/Instruction Phase

> **Step One:** The teacher selects a paragraph from an narrative or expository text to model the GIST strategy. Newspaper articles work well, but so do sections of content-area textbooks and other passages.

> **Step Two:** Have students look at the first sentence of a paragraph and identify the most important or key concepts (for news articles they list the *who, what, when, where, why,* and *how*). Ask students to write a brief summary of the sentence (fifteen words or less). The teacher writes this summary on the overhead or chalkboard.

> **Step Three:** The teacher shows students the second sentence of the paragraph and then erases the first summary statement. The teacher asks students to summarize both sentences in fifteen words or less.

> **Step Four:** Repeat this process until students have summarized the entire paragraph in fifteen words or less.

Guided Practice Phase

> **Step Five:** The teacher gives students another article or paragraph to summarize in fifteen words or less. The teacher should observe students and guide them in writing these summaries. Summaries can be done individually or in small groups. Students can share their summaries with the whole class.

Application Phase

> **Step Six:** Students should be given opportunities to practice and use the GIST summary strategy. Summarization can be tricky and ongoing practice can help reinforce this skill. Use GIST with different kinds of texts.

Adaptations

Math Word Problems: Students can use GIST to identify the key elements of a word problem. Students read the problem and tell the teacher what terms and concepts are most important. Then they list the ten to fifteen most important words (depending on the length of the problem). Students can then rewrite the problem in their own words leaving out unnecessary words from the original problem.

Web Page GIST: Students can use GIST to summarize information obtained from the Internet and other multimedia sources.

Source: Based on Cunningham, J. (1982). Generating interactions between schemata and text. In J. Niles & L. Harris (Eds.), *New inquiries in reading research and instruction, thirty-first yearbook of the National Reading Conference* (pp. 42–47). Washington, DC: National Reading Conference.

GIST Sample Exercise—Math Word Problem

Name: Jake

Topic or problem and page number:

Number sentences

Word problem

Samantha is helping her mother and father arrange bricks for a new walkway in their backyard. There 624 bricks. Samantha has to put the bricks in rows of 5 bricks. What number sentence can be used to find out how many rows of bricks Samantha can make? Will they have any bricks left over? If so, how many?

Read the word problem and list the 10 to 15 most important words/ideas in the problem:

624 bricks	walkway	rows of 5 bricks
number sentence	left over	

Write a 15-word summary:

Divide 624 bricks by 5 for the length of the walkway.

GIST with a Math Word Problem

Name: _____

Topic or problem and page number:

_____

Read the word problem and list the 10 to 15 most important words/ideas in the problem:

_____   _____   _____

_____   _____   _____

_____   _____   _____

_____   _____   _____

_____   _____   _____

Write a 15-word summary:

_____

_____

_____

_____

Copyright © 2006 Allyn and Bacon, Pearson Education, Inc.

GIST with a Newspaper Article

Name: _____

Title: _____

Source: _____ Date: _____

Read the article and answer the following:

Who?	What?	When?
Where?	Why?	How?

Write a 15-word summary:

_____

_____

_____

Copyright © 2006 Allyn and Bacon, Pearson Education, Inc.

STRATEGY 8

Anticipation Guide

Objective: To help stimulate discussion and critical thinking to enable students to better understand expository and narrative material

Rationale/Description: The Anticipation Guide is a series of teacher-generated statements that help elicit students' prior knowledge and reveal possible misconceptions about certain key concepts before reading a selection. (Variations may be called reasoning, prediction, or reaction guides.) Students use the statements to guide their reading, and they respond after reading to see if their views have changed or broadened.

Intended for: Elementary, intermediate, middle, and secondary students

Procedures:

Teacher Preparation Stage

Step One: Decide on a story, textbook selection, newspaper article, or any other material to be studied and note the key concepts and lesson objectives. Develop approximately five to ten statements, not questions, that reflect these key concepts. Make certain that the statements are sufficiently general and likely stimulate students' thinking. Type or write the statements on the blank Anticipation Guide provided and run copies for the students.

Prereading Stage

Step Two: Display the guide on an overhead projector and introduce it as a means of improving students' understanding by helping them collect all they know and can predict about a topic before reading.

Step Three: Tell them to take turns reading each of the statements with their partner, indicating whether they agree or disagree with the content. They do not have to agree with each other, but it is essential that they substantiate their answers.

Step Four: You may choose to engage in a whole class discussion of the answers in order to ascertain their level of prior knowledge or degree of misconceptions about the topic. Explain to the students that, at this point, they are free to share their thinking and predictions and that no one will be put on the spot.

Reading Stage

Step Five: Have the students read, listen to, or view the related material using the statements as their guide to the key concepts in the selection.

Postreading Stage

Step Six: After reading the selection, have the students indicate (as a class, individually, in pairs, or in small groups) whether they agree or disagree with each statement now that they have read the entire selection. It is important that students be required to discuss the reasons behind their answers, even indicating where in the text they located the answer.

Source: Based on Readence, J. E., Bean, T. W., & Baldwin, R. S. (1989). *Content area reading: An integrated approach.* Dubuque, IA: Kendall-Hunt.

Anticipation Guide Sample Exercise

Ducks Don't Get Wet by Augusta Goldin

Before   **After**

_____   1. Bird and duck feathers are waterproof.   _____

_____   2. You can easily mix oil and water together.   _____

_____   3. Most ducks don't dive very deeply.   _____

_____   4. Ducks can swim the length of a city block.   _____

_____   5. Ducks can fly as fast as an automobile.   _____

_____   6. When ducks are hungry, they fly south.   _____

Anticipation Guide Sample Exercise—
Biology, Unit on Amphibians

Before   **After**

_____   1. Most amphibians live all their lives on land.   _____

_____   2. Amphibians are vertebrates.   _____

_____   3. Amphibians evolved from fish millions of years ago.   _____

_____   4. Adult amphibians eat only vegetation.   _____

_____   5. Amphibian eggs do not have a hard shell.   _____

_____   6. Amphibians have large eyes.   _____

_____   7. Frogs do not have ears.   _____

_____   8. There are three groups of amphibians: _____

           (1.) _____   (2.) _____   (3.) _____

Anticipation Guide

Title/unit: _____

Name(s) _____

Before   **After**

_____   1. _____   _____

                      _____

_____   2. _____   _____

                      _____

_____   3. _____   _____

                      _____

_____   4. _____   _____

                      _____

_____   5. _____   _____

                      _____

_____   6. _____   _____

                      _____

_____   7. _____   _____

                      _____

_____   8. _____   _____

                      _____

_____   9. _____   _____

                      _____

_____   10. _____   _____

                      _____

Copyright © 2006 Allyn and Bacon, Pearson Education, Inc.

STRATEGY 9

KWL Plus

Objective: To elicit students' knowledge and experience before, during, and after reading to enhance their understanding and recall

Rationale/Description: This brainstorming strategy requires that students tell everything they know (K) about a topic (prereading stage), indicate what they want (W) to know more about (purpose-setting stage), tell what they learned (L) after reading the text (postreading stage), and then engage in a writing activity to express their learning (Plus). KWL Plus has its roots in the schema-theoretic view of comprehension that suggests that stimulating readers' prior knowledge (getting them to talk about their experiences), increases comprehension.

Intended for: Elementary, intermediate, middle, and secondary students

Procedures:

Prereading Stage

Step One: Explain to the students that they will engage in a brainstorming activity to get them to think about everything they know about a given topic. Remind the students that thinking about what they already know will help them better remember and understand what they read.

Step Two: Display the KWL form on an overhead projector and hand the forms out to the students. Explain the meaning of each phase.

Step Three: Ask the students to think of everything they can about a given topic to be studied. Ensure that this topic is one on which they possess at least some prior knowledge. Write the contributions of the class under section K on the form.

Step Four: Now ask the students what they want to learn about the topic based, at least in part on their previous contributions. Write these in question form under the W section of the form. The teacher may choose to add a few questions to further emphasize key concepts. Explain that these questions serve as their purposes for reading and will help them focus on the important information in the text.

Reading Stage

Step Five: Tell the students to read the selection, using the purpose-setting questions as their guide. Remember that although the example given is for a reading lesson, this strategy can be used with other types of information sources as well, such as videotapes, experiments, field trips, lectures, listening activities, and so on.

Postreading Stage

Step Six: After reading, have the students brainstorm what they recall from the text and write their contributions on the board or an overhead transparency. The teacher may choose to prompt for or add key concepts not initially mentioned.

Writing Stage

Step Seven: Help the students come up with ways to categorize the information listed in the L section by modeling a few examples. One option, shown in the example, is to use symbols (in this case, letters) to represent the categories. Then as a class, in small groups, or individually, organize the information in the form of a semantic map.

Step Eight: Pre-assign students to pairs or small groups to write about one or more of the categories. Students can work together, refer to the text, and jointly elaborate as they come up with one passage between them. It would be beneficial to think aloud a sample paragraph with the class to model this process. Pairs or groups can share their completed compositions with the class.

Source: Based on Carr, E., & Ogle, D. M. (1987). K-W-L-Plus: A strategy for comprehension and summarization. *Journal of Reading, 30,* 626–631.

KWL Plus Sample Exercise—Science

Topic: Crocodiles

1. Whole Class/Small Group Contributions

K (Know)	W (Want to Know)	L (Learned)
Many large teeth	Where do they live?	P—Lay eggs
Big, powerful tails	What do they eat?	E—Eat birds, mammals, fish
Reptiles	How are they different from alligators?	P—Can grow to 20' in length
Live in swamps	How large do they get?	P—Can stay underwater 2½ hours without air
Long, low body	Characteristics?	P—Can outrun man
Crocodile Dundee		T—American, live in Florida
		T—Nile, live in Africa
		T—Salt Water, live in India and Australia
		P—Can wrestle a buffalo
		P—Sometimes attack and devour people
		L—Prefer swamps, marshes, shallow water

2. Class/Group Constructed Semantic Map

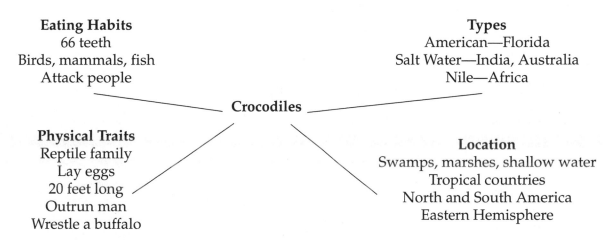

Eating Habits
66 teeth
Birds, mammals, fish
Attack people

Types
American—Florida
Salt Water—India, Australia
Nile—Africa

Crocodiles

Physical Traits
Reptile family
Lay eggs
20 feet long
Outrun man
Wrestle a buffalo

Location
Swamps, marshes, shallow water
Tropical countries
North and South America
Eastern Hemisphere

3. Sample Summary for Physical Traits

Like most reptiles, crocodiles lay eggs. They can grow to a length of 20 feet and can outrun a man while on land or wrestle and devour animals as large as a buffalo. Since crocodiles can stay under water for up to 2½ hours without coming up for air, it is not a good idea to go swimming in swampy water.

KWL Plus Sample Exercise—Math Learning about Fractions

1. **Whole Class Instruction.** Teacher introduces the concept of fractions to the whole class by cutting a peanut butter sandwich (or pie, pizza, or a paper circle). The teacher shows the whole and fractional parts as he or she cuts the sandwich. This provides a visual example and activates prior knowledge.

2. **Small Group Discussion and KWL.** Students work in small groups to discuss what they know about fractions.

K (Know)	W (Want to Know)	L (Learned)
Fractions are parts of a whole. The parts have to be the same. The parts can be added.	How many parts can you have? Do they have to be the same shape? How can we add the pieces together?	You can have many very small parts. You can add parts together (add numerators). To add you need a common denominator.

3. **Sample Summary for Fractions.** Fractions are a way of showing a smaller part of something. The fractions are like pieces that can be added together to make bigger pieces. A fraction has a top number called a numerator and a bottom number called a denominator. You can add fractions when they have the same denominator. You add them by adding the top numbers together.

KWL Plus Form

K	W	L
What we know	**What we *want* to find out**	**What we *learned***

Copyright © 2006 Allyn and Bacon, Pearson Education, Inc.

KWL Plus Writing Form

Names: _____   Date: _____

1. With your partner(s), group the information from the "What we learned" section here.

2. With your partner(s), write one or more paragraphs using the key concepts. Be sure to look back in your book if you need more information.

Copyright © 2006 Allyn and Bacon, Pearson Education, Inc.

STRATEGY 10

Collaborative Listening–Viewing Guide (CLVG)

Objective: To help students learn from visual information

Rationale/Description: The Collaborative Listening–Viewing Guide (CLVG) is a lesson framework to help students learn from information observed and/or heard. It can be used to manage and organize content learned from experiments, demonstrations, lectures, field trips, videotapes, the Internet, or other multimedia texts.

Intended for: Elementary, intermediate, middle, and secondary students and students who need additional support

Procedures:

Step One: *Preview/review information.* In this introductory phase, give an overview of the topic, preteach significant terms if needed, and elicit the students' background knowledge on the topic. This information can be organized on the board in the form of a semantic map.

Step Two: *Record individually.* Instruct the class to write down significant ideas, concepts, phrases, and so forth on the left-hand side of their paper. Students should be instructed to be brief and use abbreviations as needed. Notes should be recorded in sequential order.

Step Three: *Elaborate in small groups.* After viewing the video, have the students get in groups to elaborate on their individual notes (it is best if these heterogeneous groups are established beforehand). Here they can recall details, extend ideas, add personal anecdotes, and so on. Then they record this information on the right-hand side of their forms.

Step Four: *Synthesize with the whole class.* Tell the students to contribute what they learned from their group recollections and then record their responses on the board, chart paper, or a transparency. This information can then be reorganized as a map, chart, or outline, as appropriate.

Step Five (Optional): *Extend in pairs.* Have students work in pairs to (a) design a project related to the topic, (b) compose a paragraph synthesizing some of the information, (c) develop a chart or map of the key concepts, (d) write a play or a skit, or (e) research an aspect of the topic in more detail.

Source: Based on Wood, K. D. (1994) *Practical strategies for improving instruction.* Columbus, OH: National Middle School Association.

Collaborative Listening–Viewing Guide Sample Exercise

Name: Ryan   Group Members Tonya, Joshua, Miguel

Class: Miss Maye   Date: Jan. 28   Topic: War of 1812

We know: That in early 1800s President Jefferson didn't want war; that trade was important to us

My Notes:

- Britain took our soldiers
- War Hawks wanted war
- Indians sided with the British
- Francis Scott Key wrote anthem
- Andrew Jackson fought American war

Our Group's Notes:

- Captured our ships and men to fight in the war with France
- Said they were British citizens who deserted
- War Hawks and other Americans wanted war but some who trade with Britain weren't too happy.
- President Madison gets Congress to declare war June 18, 1812.
- Out west, Tecumseh helped British take Detroit and Chicago.
- In the east they burned the White House. Frances Scott Key wrote a poem that was set to music as our national anthem while in prison.
- Also burned other government buildings
- In south, General Jackson led Americans to defeat Britain. They lost over 1,900 soldiers in the Battle of New Orleans.

We learned: That the British left us alone, American trade improved, new factories started.

We will find out: More about President Jackson (Josh and Ryan), Tecumseh

Collaborative Web Search–Viewing Guide Sample Exercise

Student's Name: **Tameka**   Group Members: **Raul, Samantha, Michael, Rachel**

Class: **Art**   Date: **Sept. 28**   Topic: **Henri Matisse**

We know:

My Notes

- Matisse was a French artist who lived from 1869 to 1954.

- Matisse painted in many styles and used different media (painting, tapestry, stage design, paper cutouts).

- He was one of the greatest artists of the 20th century.

Our Group's Notes

- Matisse was the father of the "fauvist" movement.

- Matisse and Pablo Picasso were two of the most popular artists of the 20th century.

- Matisse painted people in domestic scenes and landscapes.

- Fauvists painted using bright colors, applied paint straight from the tubes to create a sense of an explosion of color on the canvas.

We learned: That Matisse was a French artist who was very important during the 20th century. His work is very valuable today and he has influenced many other artists.

We will find out: Some examples of his art so that we can try to paint in his style. We'd also like to know more about Picasso and compare his art to Matisse's.

Collaborative Listing–Viewing Guide Form

Student's Name: _____   Group Members: _____

Class: _____   Date: _____   Topic: _____

We know:

My Notes   **Our Group's Notes**

We learned:

We will find out:

Copyright © 2006 Allyn and Bacon, Pearson Education, Inc.

STRATEGY 11

Inquiry Charts (I-Charts)

Objective: To help teachers and students organize new information from multiple sources

Rationale/Description: Inquiry Charts are designed to nurture critical reading in content classrooms by having students examine multiple sources of information. The chart allows students to gather information from varied sources and organize it for summarization, comparison, analysis, and evaluation.

Intended for: Elementary, intermediate, middle, and secondary students

Procedures:

Step One: Decide on the topic, questions, or sources that relate to the topic just covered or introduced. Type or handwrite significant questions across the top of the blank I-Chart that follows. Then make an overhead and copies for students (if desired).

Step Two: Introduce the I-Chart as a means of organizing what students already know as well as what they will learn or have learned regarding the topic being studied.

Step Three: Students and teacher share prior knowledge, experiences, and facts and fill in each question across the top of the chart.

Step Four: The class can work as a whole or can be divided into groups to search various sources for information related to the topic. For example, groups of four or five may search online encyclopedias and websites, while other groups go the textbook or tradebooks for information.

Step Five: The class or groups can then synthesize the information in the form of summary statements at the bottom of each column. As students become more proficient in composing short summaries they can be asked to work in pairs or individually to expand them into paragraphs and written reports.

Step Six: Students can be asked to compare new information with prior knowledge and reconcile any previous misconceptions.

Step Seven (Optional): The I-Chart can be conducted first as a whole class activity and then the responsibility can be turned over to small groups, pairs, and eventually individuals to complete the data collection.

Source: Based on Hoffman, J. V. (1992). Critical reading/thinking across the curriculum: Using I-charts to support learning. *Language Arts, 69,* 121–127.

I-Chart Sample Exercise—The Industrial Revolution

Topic The Industrial Revolution	Guiding Questions				Interesting facts and figures	New questions
	1. What new technologies started the revolution?	2. What was the political situation like at this time?	3. How did artists react to the changes in society (through literature, music, and the visual arts)?	4. How did these changes affect the general population?		
What We Know	Machines were used to manufacture many items.	Socialism began to gain popularity.	Many artists focused on the negative aspects of life.	The quality of life improved in some ways, but worsened in other ways.		
Source 1: Class text	Communication and transportation were areas of development.	Social Reformism began	Romanticism, Impressionism, and Realism were important styles.	Pollution became a problem.	Young children were forced to work 14 hour shifts in factories!	
Source 2: Encyclopedias	Textiles and iron production were important industries.	The 1867 Reform Act gave many working men the right to vote.	Van Gogh used vibrant colors to show his unhappiness.	Prices dropped: many items became available to all.		
Source 3: Library trade book			C. Dickens wrote novels describing poor working conditions.	Working conditions were harsh for men, women, and children.		
Source 4: Internet/ Multimedia	New machines greatly improved manufacturing.	Began in a time of revolution—French and American.	Artists like Delacroix began to celebrate the individual.			
Summary						

I-Chart Form

Topic	Guiding Questions				Interesting facts and figures	New questions
	1.	2.	3.	4.		
What we know						
Source 1:						
Source 2:						
Source 3:						
Source 4:						
Summary						

Copyright © 2006 Allyn and Bacon, Pearson Education, Inc.

STRATEGY 12

Possible Sentences

Objective: To help reinforce the understanding and recall of key concepts

Rationale/Description: Possible Sentences provides direct instruction on the unfamiliar vocabulary of a reading selection by drawing on students' existing knowledge of the new vocabulary. The main purpose of this strategy is to assist students in independently determining the meanings and relationships of new words by using the context of the reading selection. Because students use their prior knowledge to predict relationships among new vocabulary items, their motivation to read the assignment is increased and a mental set is developed for reading the new material.

Intended for: Elementary, intermediate, middle, and secondary students

Procedures:

Step One: Select key vocabulary words from a content area textbook selection, trade book, short story, basal reader, or newspaper article to be read (approximately six to eight for beginning or struggling readers and ten to fifteen for average and above readers). These terms should reflect the major concepts in the selection and may include a combination of new, somewhat familiar, and very familiar terms.

Prereading Stage

Step Two: Visually display the key terms of the selection on the chalkboard, poster paper, or the overhead projector and have the students pronounce each term after the teacher. (The blank form included can be used to display the terms via transparency and to make copies for students as well.) Teacher and students should discuss the meaning of each term by making associations (synonyms), for example.

Step Three: Ask the students to compose a sentence that uses two of these vocabulary words that they think may *possibly* appear in the selection to be read. (It is important to emphasize that the sentences not be personal, e.g., "I know someone that pollutes the environment." Instead, they should be similar in style and format to the selection under study. The teacher may want to model an example.) Write each sentence on the board or overhead exactly as dictated by the students, even though the information may be inaccurate. Continue this procedure until the students are unable to produce any more sentences.

Reading Stage

Step Four: Tell the students that they are to read the assigned selection with these sentences as their guides. They are to read to either confirm or refute the information reflected in the sentences. Using the blank form, have the students write T if they believe the sentence is true, F if they believe it is false, and DK if they do not know whether a sentence is true or false. It is not necessary for them to copy these sentences on their paper, since the sentences may not be true.

Postreading Stage

Step Five: As an oral or written activity (depending on time constraints) for the whole class or for groups, have students make the necessary revisions in the existing sentences to comply with the selection they read—that is, to rewrite the sentences to make them true. Should disagreements emerge, have the students refer to the text.

Step Six: After the final modifications have been completed, the teacher may have the students record the sentences on the blank form to assist them later with the vocabulary and key concepts being studied.

Step Seven (Optional): Have the students go back to the key concepts after the exercise and review meanings.

ELL TIP: ■ *The Possible Sentences strategy can be adapted for use with English language learners and second language learners. Have students write vocabulary words in both languages and then create sentences in one or both languages. It is best to work with fewer words (5 or 6) at one time since students will be working in two languages.*

Source: Based on Moore, D. W., & Moore, S. A. (1986). Possible sentences. In E. K. Dishner, T. W. Bean, J. E. Readence, & D. W. Moore (Eds.), *Reading in the content areas: Improving classroom instruction* (2nd ed.). Dubuque, IA: Kendall/Hunt.

Possible Sentences Sample Exercise—Science

Topic: Pollution

1. Vocabulary words

environment	sulfur
pollution	sanitary landfills
exhaust	billboard
custodians	electricity
chlorine	smog
carbon monoxide	recycling

2. Student-generated possible sentences (before reading) and postreading reactions (T = true, F = false, DK = don't know)

_____ 1. Pollution is dangerous to our health.

_____ 2. Electricity is one way to get rid of pollution in the environment.

_____ 3. Too much chlorine in the air is bad for your lungs.

_____ 4. The smog makes it hard to breathe.

_____ 5. Billboards often say not to pollute.

_____ 6. Custodians work in schools to keep them clean.

_____ 7. The exhaust from a car is called carbon monoxide.

_____ 8. Too much recycling causes pollution.

_____ 9. Sulfer is caused by factory pollution.

3. Modified sentences

_____ 1. Pollution is dangerous to our health.

_____ 2. We can help stop pollution by using electricity wisely.

_____ 3. Water treated with chlorine, which kills bacteria, makes it safe to drink.

_____ 4. Gases, smoke, and moisture form smog, which makes it hard for us to see distances.

_____ 5. Billboards and junkyards spoil the natural beauty of the land.

_____ 6. Custodians work in schools, hospitals, and other buildings to keep them clean.

_____ 7. The exhaust from a car is called carbon monoxide and is one of the most dangerous pollutants.

_____ 8. Paper, glass, and metal can be collected for recycling—using over again.

_____ 9. Sulfer is a pollutant caused by nature and is sometimes found in spring water. It makes water unhealthy to drink and makes it smell bad.

Possible Sentences Sample Exercise—Reading/Language Arts

Freckle Juice **by Judy Blume**

1. **Vocabulary words**

   refrigerator   mayonnaise   greenish
   gulped   absolutely   moaned
   stomach   awful   mistake
   vinegar   decorated   probably
   ketchup   Andrew Marcus

2. **Student generated possible sentences (before reading) and postreading reactions (T = true, F = false, DK = don't know)**

   _____ 1. Andrew Marcus probably put vinegar in the formula by mistake.

   _____ 2. He put the secret formula in the refrigerator to keep the mayonnaise cold.

   _____ 3. The freckle juice he gulped was greenish in color.

   _____ 4. The recipe for freckle juice contained vinegar, ketchup, and mayonnaise.

   _____ 5. Andrew Marcus moaned after drinking the juice.

   _____ 6. The juice he put in his stomach tasted absolutely awful.

   _____ 7. Jars of mayonnaise and ketchup decorated the refrigerator shelves.

3. **Modified sentences**

   _____ 1. Andrew Marcus dropped a lemon seed in the formula by mistake.

   _____ 2. He found everything on the shelves except the lemon and onion that were in the refrigerator.

   _____ 3. Andrew turned greenish and felt very sick.

   _____ 4. The recipe for freckle juice contained vinegar, ketchup, and mayonnaise as well as lemon, pepper, salt, olive oil, onion, grape juice, and mustard.

   _____ 5. Andrew Marcus moaned after drinking the juice.

   _____ 6. The juice he put in his stomach tasted absolutely awful.

   _____ 7. Andrew studied his reflection in the mirror and decorated his face with a magic marker.

Possible Sentences Form

1. **Write the key concepts here:**

   _____   _____   _____   _____

   _____   _____   _____   _____

   _____   _____   _____   _____

   _____   _____   _____   _____

2. **Possible sentences and postreading reactions (T = true, F = false, DK = don't know)**

   1. _____

   2. _____

   3. _____

   4. _____

   5. _____

   6. _____

   7. _____

   8. _____

   9. _____

   10. _____

3. **Modified sentences**

   1. _____

   2. _____

   3. _____

   4. _____

   Copyright © 2006 Allyn and Bacon, Pearson Education, Inc.

5. _____

6. _____

7. _____

8. _____

9. _____

10. _____

Copyright © 2006 Allyn and Bacon, Pearson Education, Inc.

STRATEGY 13

Exchange Compare Writing

Objective: To reinforce key vocabulary through writing and prediction

Rationale/Description: In this strategy, students use the teacher-selected key concepts to predict the content of the chapter, literature selection, or passage to be studied. Students collaborate with peers to reinforce their understanding of key concepts while simultaneously engaging in a writing exercise.

Intended for: Elementary, intermediate, middle and secondary students

Procedures:

Preparation Phase

Step One: Determine ten to fifteen (or six to eight, depending upon the grade and ability levels of the students) significant terms from a basal story—content area selection, newspaper article, and so on—that reflect the most important information. Write or type these terms on the spaces provided with the corresponding form. Pre-assign the students to heterogeneous groups of four or five.

Prereading Stage

Step Two: Use an overhead projector to display the terms and hand out a copy to the students. Have the students pronounce the words after you in case some of the terms are in their listening but not their reading vocabulary. Tell them that they are to use these terms to predict the content of the selection to be studied.

Step Three: Have the students work in their small groups to engage in a communal writing exercise—that is, putting their heads together in the composition of a single product. They should be instructed to guess how the words may be used to convey the information in the selection to be read.

Step Four: If assistance with definitions is needed, use the word in a sentence to help students with the context clues or have them look up the word in a dictionary.

Step Five: Circulate among the groups to monitor and provide assistance. An optional step is to have the students engage in peer editing groups (described in the beginning of this book) to further polish their compositions.

Step Six: Have the groups share their completed compositions orally with the class as a means of stimulating their interest in the selection to follow.

Reading Stage

Step Seven: Have the students read the passage silently, orally, or a combination of both methods, being certain to focus on the way the significant terms are used in the selection.

Postreading Stage

Step Eight: Engage the students in a discussion of the way the terms were used in the actual selection. An option is to further reinforce the new concepts by having students use the key concepts in a composition that reflects or summarizes the actual passage.

Source: Based on Wood, K. D. (1994). *Practical strategies for improving instruction.* Columbus, OH: National Middle School Association.

Exchange Compare Writing Sample Exercise

1. **Key concepts/phrases**

   ### The Ice Age

600 million years ago	southward
glaciers and ice sheets	arctic musk oxen
oceans	woolly mammoths
Great Lakes	died out
horse	change in climate
camel	moraines
elephant	New York

2. **Predicted passage**

   The Ice Age started over *600 million years ago* when *glaciers and ice sheets* took over the *oceans*. There were no glaciers on the *Great Lakes* or in *New York*. *Arctic musk oxen* and *woolly mammoths died out* when the ice melted and caused a *change in climate*. They went *southward* to the *moraines*. Later, the *horse, camel,* and *elephant* appeared on the Earth.

3. **Passage based on actual selection**

   The earliest period in the Earth's history, when *glaciers* and *ice sheets* covered the Earth, began over *600 million years ago*. As the glaciers melted, low areas filled with water. That is how the *Great Lakes* and the *oceans* were formed. Some of the soil and rocks left behind formed ridges called *moraines*.

   The modern *horse, camel,* and *elephant* appeared during the Ice Age. When the ice melted, the animals went *southward*. *Arctic musk oxen* and *woolly mammoths* lived as far south as Michigan and *New York*. Some scientists think the *change in climate* caused some of these large mammals to *die out*. Others think they were killed by human beings.

Exchange Compare Writing Form

Group members: _____

Part 1: Predict how the terms below might be used in selection to be read.

_____	_____	_____	_____
_____	_____	_____	_____
_____	_____	_____	_____
_____	_____	_____	_____

Part 2: Write your predicted passage in the space below.

Part 3: Read the selection and use the terms again in another passage.

Copyright © 2006 Allyn and Bacon, Pearson Education, Inc.

STRATEGY 14

Paired Reading for Fluency

Objective: To help students improve the smoothness of their reading, while simultaneously reinforcing key concepts

Rationale/Description: In order to ensure that the reading ability of beginning or struggling readers improves, it is necessary to give them ample opportunities throughout the day to practice fluency. Students reading challenging texts such as historical documents or older literary texts can also benefit from improving fluency. English language learners and second language learners need work on fluency as well. Fluency is the ability to read material with few interruptions due to inadequate word attack or word recognition problems. Paired reading is one strategy that is designed to help students develop reading fluency by giving them practice with peers. For many students, fluency practice should take place at least once a day and should last approximately fifteen to twenty minutes.

Intended for: Elementary, middle, and secondary students and students who need additional support

Procedures:

Preparation Phase

Step One: Make sure that materials are available to practice fluency. These passages or books should be short—25 or 50–100 words, depending on the ability levels of the students. They should also be passages that pose no comprehension problems for the students, since the purpose of the assignment is to practice fluency. Short workbook segments or tradebook excerpts written at low levels are usually appropriate. Passages that are related to the content being studied are especially useful to reinforce learning the key concepts while practicing reading skills. Articles from children's and teen magazines are also good sources.

Step Two: Pre-assign the struggling or beginning readers to pairs, making certain that the students are at similar ability levels so that they can mutually benefit from peer instruction. Tell them that the purpose of this assignment is to help them become better readers and that improving the ability to read, as with any activity or sport, requires that they practice each day.

Step Three: Students first read their passages silently and then decide who will practice reading first. Students alternate the roles of reader and listener throughout the practice session.

Step Four: When asked to serve as reader, the student reads the passage aloud to the partner three different times. The partner can assist with pronunciation and meaning if needed. Then the reader engages in a self-evaluation, answering the question "How well did you read?" When asked to serve as the listener, the student listens to the partner's reading and then notes how the reading improved on the evaluation form. Note that the only opportunity for partners to evaluate one another is to give a positive response, not a negative one.

Step Five: After the third reading, the students switch roles and go back to Step Three. Teachers should circulate among the dyads to provide assistance, take notes (either mental or written), and model effective fluent reading for the students.

ELL TIP: ■ *Partner Reading works well with English language learners and second language learners. For ELL students, choose texts that are written in both the student's first language and English. Students can work on the text first in their native language and then work on improving fluency in English. For SLL students, have students work with texts in the second language.*

Source: Wood, K. D. (1998). Helping struggling readers read. *Middle School Journal, 29*(5), 67–70. Adapted from Koskinen, P. S., & Blum, I. H. (1986). Paired repeated reading: A classroom strategy for developing fluent reading. *The Reading Teacher, 40*(1), 70–75. Reprinted with permission of Karen Wood and the National Middle School Association.

Partner Reading Assessment

Name: _____   Partner: _____

Date: _____   We read: _____

Reading #1

How well did you read?   **Score!**   **Good**   **OK**   **Try Again**

Reading #2

How well did you read?

Reading #3

How well did you read?

How did your partner's reading improve?

_____ Read more smoothly

_____ Knew more words

_____ Read with more expression

Tell your partner one thing that was better about his or her reading: _____

_____

_____

_____

Copyright © 2006 Allyn and Bacon, Pearson Education, Inc.

STRATEGY 15

Probable Passages

Objective: To reinforce students' knowledge and understanding by using key concepts, prediction, and writing

Rational/Description: In Probable Passages, students use their knowledge of how stories are structured, as well as their inferencing abilities, to predict the content of selections to be read. Six major story grammar elements are typically found in stories in our western culture: (1) setting (introduction of characters, time and location), (2) beginning (a precipitating event), (3) reaction (main character's responses to the beginning or the formation of a goal), (4) attempt (plan to reach a goal), (5) outcome (success or failure of attempt), and (6) ending (long range consequences). Students use key concepts from a selection in a class constructed passage, reflecting their predictions about the story. This collaborative approach to composition models the writing process for less proficient writers and allows the teacher to emphasize vocabulary, comprehension, and writing within a single lesson.

Intended for: Elementary, intermediate, middle, and secondary students and students who need additional support

Procedures:

Preparation Stage

> **Step One:** Analyze the selection for the most significant concepts, terms, or names that reflect the key ideas and events, and present these on the board or an overhead projector.

> **Step Two:** Display the blank concept frame that lists the story structure elements at the top and the incomplete probable passage at the bottom. (Note that these elements can be changed to coordinate with story type.)

Prereading Stage

> **Step Three:** Tell the students that they are going to be engaged in a strategy to help them use the key vocabulary words in a story to predict what the story is probably about. Tell them this strategy is designed to help them improve their vocabulary, comprehension, and writing skills.

> **Step Four:** After reading the words with the students, tell the class to use the words to mentally construct a story line. Then, as a class, put the words in the appropriate categories. Tell them that some words may fit in more than one category and that they can fill in with other words not listed that their background

knowledge suggests may be feasible. (See words in parentheses in the sample lesson.)

Step Five: Direct the class's attention to each line of the story frame and have them use the words to develop a logical, probable passage.

Reading Stage

Step Six: Have the students read the selection individually or in pairs with their predicted story lines in mind.

Postreading Stage

Step Eight: After reading and discussing the story, have the class make the necessary changes on the key concept frame.

Step Nine: Have the class modify the probable passage to reflect the actual events of the selection.

Step Ten (Optional): After more than one experience with this strategy as a class, students can work in small groups or pairs to construct probable and actual passages for other stories. They can share their probable passages with other groups to note the range of alternatives.

> **ELL TIP:** ■ *Probable Passages can be adapted for use with English Language Learners (ELL) and Second Language Learners (SLL). For both groups, teachers should take care to select fewer terms that are within reach of these students. Students can work in small groups or as a whole class to construct the story line. Also, for use with any group of struggling or emerging readers, teachers can help students place terms in the correct category (setting, characters, problem, solution, ending).*

Source: Based on Wood, K. D. (1984, February). Probable passages: A writing strategy. *The Reading Teacher,* 37(6), 496–499.

Key Concept Frame Sample Exercise

Setting	Character(s)	Problem	Solution	Ending
doughnut shop bakery	Tomas (a little boy) Mr. Tucker (owner of shop)	whirr buzz clunk machine flour huge start button	bank loan invented customer money	delicious jelly-cinnamon-honey doughnut

Sample Probable Passage

The story takes place in a *doughnut shop. Mr. Tucker* is a character in the story who *owns the store.* A problem occurs when *Tomas, a little boy,* pushes the *start button.* After that, the *machine* goes *whirr, buzz, and clunk* and a *huge doughnut* pops out. Next, a *customer* comes in. The problem is solved when they are given a *bank loan* and *Mr. Tucker* and *Tomas invent a way* to stop the *machine.* The story ends when *Tomas* eats a *delicious jelly-cinnamon-honey doughnut.*

Actual Passage After Reading

The story takes place in a *doughnut shop. Tomas* is the character who *invented* the *jelly-cinnamon-honey doughnut. Mr. Tucker* is the *owner of the store.* A problem occurs when *Tomas* pushes the *start-button* and can't figure out how to stop the *machine.* After that, he pushes all the buttons together, the *machine* goes *whirr, buzz, and clunk* and a huge, *jelly-cinnamon-honey doughnut* pops out. Next, Mr. Redstone, a *customer,* comes in and buys all the doughnuts. The problem is solved when *customers* come from all around to buy the doughnuts and *Mr. Tucker* doesn't have to take out a *bank loan.* The story ends when *Mr. Tucker* lets *Tomas* have a free *jelly-cinnamon-honey doughnut* every day.

Source: Wood, K. D. (1984, February). Probable passages: A writing strategy. *The Reading Teacher, 37*(6), 496–499. Copyright by the International Reading Association. Reprinted with permission from the International Reading Association.

Concept Frame

Setting	Character(s)	Problem	Solution	Ending

Passage Form

The story takes place _____ .

_____ is a character in the story who _____

_____ . A problem occurs when _____

_____ .

After that, _____

_____ .

Next, _____

_____ .

The problem is solved when _____

_____ .

The story ends _____

_____ .

   Copyright © 2006 Allyn and Bacon, Pearson Education, Inc.

STRATEGY 16

Herringbone Technique

Objective: To provide a structured outline to help students attend to significant information in a text selection (e.g., chapter) and to assist them in organizing a written response using this information

Rationale/Description: The Herringbone Technique enables students to remember important information presented in a chapter through the use of the following six important questions: Who? What? When? Where? Why? and How? The teacher provides an outline on which the students can structure their notetaking and record this information. The students can refer to their outlines for future study.

Intended for: Upper elementary, intermediate, middle, and secondary students

Procedures:

Step One: After the class has been thoroughly introduced to the target selection, the Herringbone Technique can be introduced. This can be done by reproducing the blank form and presenting one copy on the overhead projector.

Step Two: Walk through the form with the students, thinking aloud the answers for a sample of the text to model the process. Consider expanding the six questions to coordinate with the specific information in the selection.

Step Three: Provide guided practice by having the students work in pairs to begin reading and recording the significant information. Circulate and monitor the dyads to provide assistance.

Step Four: Show the students how to take the recorded information and put it in written paragraph form by talking aloud the process. Then, have them practice on additional textbook selections for continued improvement.

Source: Based on Herber, H. L. (1978). *Teaching reading in content areas* (2nd ed.). Englewood Cliffs, NJ: Prentice Hall.

Herringbone Technique Sample Exercise—Science

Topic: Photosynthesis

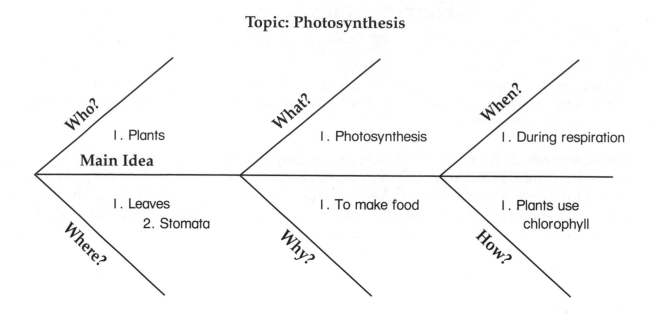

1. **Who?**   All plants

2. **What?**   Use light from the sun (and water and carbon dioxide), to produce food through the process of photosynthesis.

3. **When?**   During respiration (or breathing). In other words, almost constantly.

4. **Where?**   In the leaves, and through the stomata.

5. **Why?**   Plants use sugars for life activities, such as growth. Plants use some oxygen, and release the rest to be used by other organisms (like humans!) for breathing. Carbon dioxide is produced by other animals and is used by plants to make food. This never-ending cycle provides energy for all living things.

6. **How?**   Chlorophyll is a green pigment in plants that traps light from the sun. This sunlight is changed into energy.

Written Summary

All plants use sugars (food) as energy to grow and complete other life activities. Unlike humans, plants can make their own food. By collecting water from the ground, carbon dioxide from the air, and light from the sun, they can produce the food they need through the process of photosynthesis.

The most important part of photosynthesis is sunlight. To capture sunlight, plants must use a special substance called chlorophyll. Chlorophyll is a green pigment in plants that traps light from the sun. This sunlight is then changed into energy, in the form of sugar and oxygen. Some of the sugar and oxygen that plants make is used, some is stored for later.

Photosynthesis takes place during respiration, or whenever the plant breathes. In other words, it happens almost constantly. As carbon dioxide is produced by animals and people, it is collected and used by plants to make food. Then, the oxygen that is not used by the plant is released through the stomata to be used by other organisms (like humans!) for breathing. This never-ending cycle provides energy for all living things.

Herringbone Activity

Name:_____ Partner(s): _____

1. Read the selection and fill in the form below.

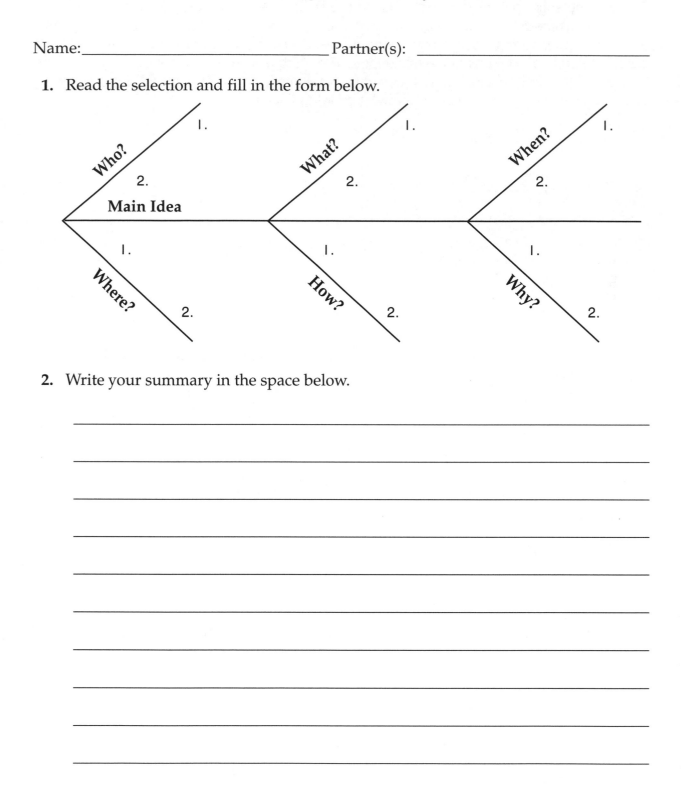

2. Write your summary in the space below.

_____

_____

_____

_____

_____

_____

_____

_____

_____

_____

Copyright © 2006 Allyn and Bacon, Pearson Education, Inc.

STRATEGY 17

Think, Pair, Share

Objective: To give students ample time to formulate an answer and undertake a learning task that involves discussion and sharing with a partner and the whole class

Rationale/Description: Think, Pair, Share is a discussion strategy in which students think individually and share with classmates how to answer a question, solve a problem, or undertake a learning task. It is a preferred alternative to calling on individual students randomly in a class and expecting them to answer on the spot. The act of discussing their thinking with a partner serves a kind of dress rehearsal before they are asked to go public with their responses in front of the class. It is also useful to engage in a Think, Pair, Share activity when students are not responding to a question. The act of discussing an answer with a partner serves to maximize participation, focus students' attention, and engage them in the learning task.

Intended for: Elementary, intermediate, middle, and secondary students and students who need additional support

Procedures:

Step One: Discuss the purpose of the collaborative strategy as a discussion starter—a means of stimulating their thinking and prior knowledge on a topic. One useful option is to display the steps of the strategy on a poster in the room to cue each phrase along the way.

Step Two: Pose a question or a problem then give the students ample time to think about their responses and jot them down on their Think, Pair, Share Think Sheet.

Step Three: Then have students pair up with pre-assigned partners or someone seated nearby to discuss their thinking. Students should write down their partners' responses on the form.

Step Four: Tell the students to share their thinking with the entire class. Newly learned answers and additional responses can be written on the Think Sheet for future referral.

Source: Based on Kagan, S. (1994). *Cooperative learning.* San Juan Capistrano, CA: Kagan Cooperative Learning.

Think, Pair, Share Sample Exercise

Name:_____ Partner: _____

1. By yourself, think about what some of the consequences would be if it was possible to control the weather? Write your notes here.

   It could be sunny all the time and we could go swimming without worrying about rainy weather. The only problem is the beaches would probably get crowded.

2. Share your thinking with a partner. Write your shared notes here.

   The other problem is that, without rain, no plants or trees could grow. People who couldn't stand hot weather would have a problem. There could be more problems with skin cancer if it got too hot.

3. Share your ideas with the class. Write down some new things you have learned.

   If the wrong people controlled the weather, they could wipe out an entire continent through storms, tornadoes, and hurricanes. It could be positive if it could be used to improve the environment and help farmers with their crops. Some people would have to make changes in the type of house they built. They'd have to be careful not to make it too hot where there are snow-topped mountains or glaciers or else there would be flooding.

Think, Pair, Share Think Sheet

Name:_____ Partner: _____

1. By yourself think about _____ .
    Write your notes here.

2. Share your thinking with a partner. Write your shared notes here.

3. Share your ideas with the class. Write down some new things you have learned.

Copyright © 2006 Allyn and Bacon, Pearson Education, Inc.

STRATEGY 18

Double Entry Journal

Objective: To help students reflect on and process new information from both print and nonprint sources

Rationale/Description: The Double Entry Journal, useful for both expository and narrative material, is also called the dialectic, dialogue, or two-column journal. It is a system of note taking in which the learner essentially engages in a discussion with the author, reflecting about and questioning specific information. Notes about the text or viewed material are written in the left-side of the paper in the What the Author Said section. Notes on the learner's personal responses are written in the What You Say section.

Intended for: Elementary, intermediate, middle, and secondary students

Procedures:

Modeling/Demonstration Phase

> **Step One:** Display the blank form on an overhead projector and explain to the students that they will learn a way to take notes that involves talking with the author and asking questions, making analogies, and expressing thoughts and reactions to the content or events.

> **Step Two:** Display either the narrative or expository example and walk the students through the some of the sample questions and comments.

> **Step Three:** Use a sample passage and talk aloud some possible responses, enlisting the aid of the class in the process.

Guided Practice Phase

> **Step Four:** Use another sample passage and divide the class into heterogeneous groups or pairs to engage in the double entry journal process. Circulate among the groups to provide assistance.

> **Step Five:** Have the groups share their journals with the entire class. Direct the students' attention to the fact that their notes in the What the Author Said portion are often very similar, but that the responses are more personal and individual in the What You say section.

Independent Practice Phase

Step Six: Allow the students to work in pairs or individually to try out the procedure independently.

Application Phase

Step Seven: Have the students apply the note-taking procedure to other subjects as well.

Source: Based on Schatzberg-Smith, K. (1989). Dialectic notes: Learner-driven interaction with text. Language Connections: A Newsletter of the Reading/Communications Resource Center. Hempstead, NY: Hofstra University.

Double Entry Journal Sample Exercise—Fiction

The Gunnywolf

What the Author Said	What You Say
Setting, time, place: The deep dark woods **Main characters (name, role, traits):** Little Girl liked to pick flowers The Gunnywolf liked to scare people **Main events (plot, problem/conflict, building action, climax, resolution):** Everytime she sings her song, it puts the wolf to sleep. **Theme (What is the author trying to get you to think about?):** Sometimes we can control our fears more than we think. **Quotable quotes:** Un-ka-cha, pit-a-pat "Sing that good, sweet song song again."	**Questions you want to ask:** Why would she take a chance going in the dark woods with a wolf? **Statements that start with *but* or *however*:** On page 98, it says "but one day she saw a flower in the woods and forgot all about the wolf"—that's why she went deeper in the woods. **Consequences (What might the characters do next if the story continues?):** I think the wolf and little girl will be friends as long as she keeps on singing. **Experiences you have had or stories that are similar:** This reminds me of Little Red Riding Hood and Lon Po Po. **Other themes:** It's still not a good idea to walk in the woods alone. **Evaluation (Would you encourage a friend to read this? Explain.):** Yes, it was fun to read the crazy words and it had a happy ending.

Double Entry Journal for Fiction

What the Author Said	What You Say
Setting, time, place:	Questions you want to ask:
Main characters (name, role, traits):	Statements that start with *but* or *however*:
Main events (plot, problem/conflict, building action, climax, resolution):	Consequences (What might the characters do next if the story continues?):
Theme (What is the author trying to get you to think about?):	Experiences you have had or stories that are similar:
Quotable quotes:	Other themes:
	Evaluation (Would you encourage a friend to read This? Explain.):

Copyright © 2006 Allyn and Bacon, Pearson Education, Inc.

Double Entry Journal for Non-Fiction

What the Author Said	What You Say
Author's main points:	Questions you want to ask:
Important details:	Statements that start with *but* or *however*:
Quotable quotes:	Suggestions—ideas the author should have discussed, but didn't:
Author's conclusions:	Other knowledge or experience you have on the topic:
Details:	Evaluation—reasons you agree or disagree with the author:
	Consequences—results or effects of the author's ideas:

Copyright © 2006 Allyn and Bacon, Pearson Education, Inc.

STRATEGY 19

Discussion Webs

Objective: To help students consider the information they read from more than one point of view

Rationale/Description: Discussion Webs are a during-reading or post-reading activities that encourage students to engage in the text and engage each other in thoughtful discussion. Discussion webs create a framework for students to explore texts and consider different sides of an issue in discussion before drawing conclusions. Discussion Webs are an alternative to teacher-dominated discussions and help activate prior knowledge and make predictions about the text. This activity can also help students who are not comfortable participating in large-group discussions talk with a partner or small group.

Intended for: Intermediate, middle, and secondary students

Procedures:

Step One: The teacher helps prepare students for reading by activating prior knowledge, raising questions, and making predictions about the text.

Step Two: The teacher assigns students to read the selection and then introduces the Discussion Web by having the students work in pairs to generate pro and con responses to the question. The partners work on the same Discussion Web and take turns jotting down their reasons in the Yes and No columns. Students may use keywords and phrases to express their ideas and need not fill all of the lines. They should try to list an equal number of pro and con responses on the web.

Step Three: Partners join another group and the four students compare responses, work toward consensus, and read a conclusion as a group. The teacher explains to students that it is okay to disagree with other members of the group, but they should all try to keep an open mind as they listen to others during the discussion. Dissenting views may be aired during the whole-class discussion.

Step Four: Each group gets three minutes to decide which of the reasons given best supports the group's conclusion. Each group selects a spokesperson to report to the whole class.

Step Five: Students follow up the whole-class discussion by individually writing their responses to the discussion web question. Display the students' responses to the question in a prominent place in the room so that they can be read by others.

Source: Based on Alvermann, D. (1992). The discussion web: A graphic aid for learning across the curriculum. *The Reading Teacher, 45,* 92–99.

Discussion Web Sample Exercise—Science

Use a Discussion Web to explore the topic of global warming.

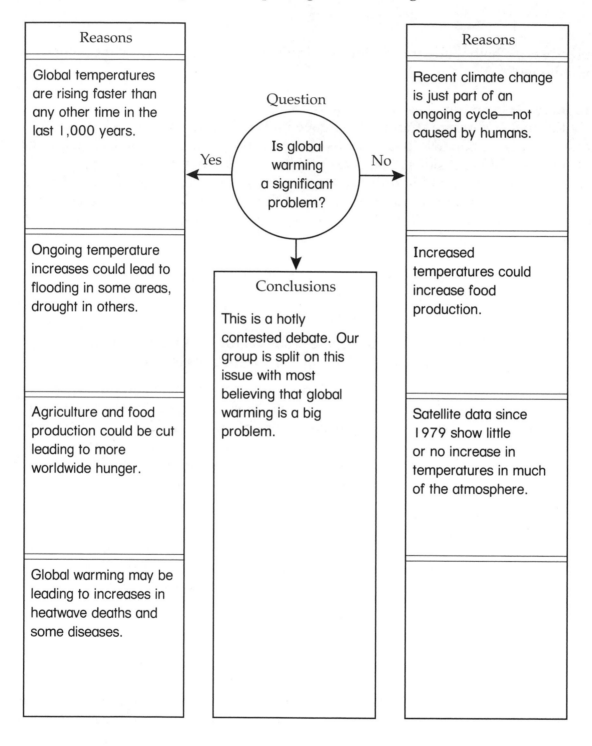

Reasons	Question	Reasons
Global temperatures are rising faster than any other time in the last 1,000 years.		Recent climate change is just part of an ongoing cycle—not caused by humans.

Yes ← **Is global warming a significant problem?** → No

Reasons	Reasons
Ongoing temperature increases could lead to flooding in some areas, drought in others.	Increased temperatures could increase food production.
Agriculture and food production could be cut leading to more worldwide hunger.	Satellite data since 1979 show little or no increase in temperatures in much of the atmosphere.
Global warming may be leading to increases in heatwave deaths and some diseases.	

Conclusions

This is a hotly contested debate. Our group is split on this issue with most believing that global warming is a big problem.

Copyright © 2006 Allyn and Bacon, Pearson Education, Inc.

Discussion Web Sample Exercise—Literature

Use a Discussion Web to explore the state of the American dream in F. Scott Fitzgerald's *The Great Gatsby*.

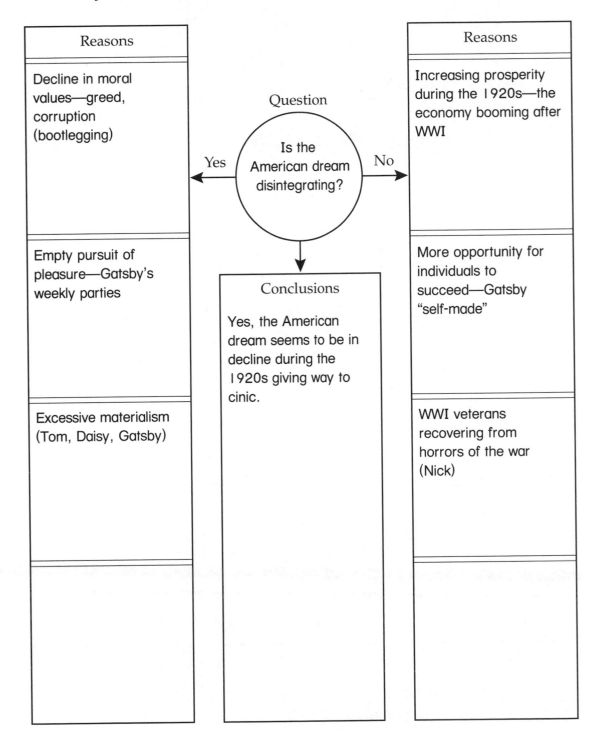

Reasons
Decline in moral values—greed, corruption (bootlegging)
Empty pursuit of pleasure—Gatsby's weekly parties
Excessive materialism (Tom, Daisy, Gatsby)

Question

Yes ← Is the American dream disintegrating? → No

Conclusions

Yes, the American dream seems to be in decline during the 1920s giving way to cinic.

Reasons
Increasing prosperity during the 1920s—the economy booming after WWI
More opportunity for individuals to succeed—Gatsby "self-made"
WWI veterans recovering from horrors of the war (Nick)

Discussion Web

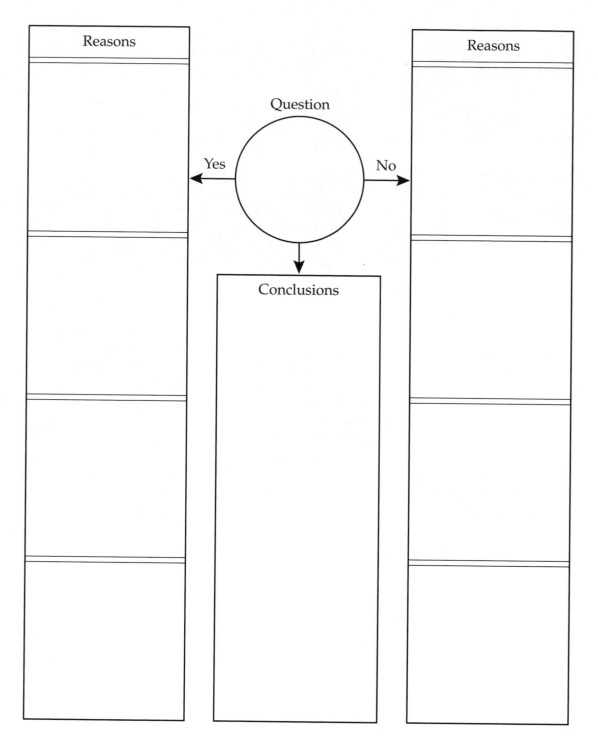

Reasons

Question

Yes

No

Conclusions

Reasons

STRATEGY 20

Imagine, Elaborate, Predict, and Confirm (IEPC)

Objective: To encourage students to use visual imagery as a means of enriching their understanding of information that is viewed, listened to, or read

Rationale/Description: IEPC is a strategy to help students increase their understanding and recall by using visual imagery to predict events in a selection. It begins by modeling for students how to imagine a scene, how to add details, and how to use their thinking to predict a possible story line. After reading, students return to confirm or disprove their original predictions. The specific components of IEPC are

- **Imagine.** Close your eyes and try to imagine the scene. Share your thinking with a partner and the whole class.
- **Elaborate.** Think of details surrounding the scene in your head. How do you think the characters feel? What are similar experiences? Describe the scene. What do you see, feel, hear, smell?
- **Predict.** Use what you have imagined in your head to predict what might happen in the story (characters, events, setting, etc.).
- **Confirm.** During and after reading the selection, think about your original predictions. Were they true, false, or were they not explained in the passage? Modify your predictions to coordinate with the actual selection.

Intended for: Elementary, middle, and secondary students

Procedures:

Modeling Phase

> **Step One:** Decide on an appropriate tradebook, basal selection, or passage with content appropriate for developing imagery.

> **Step Two:** Display the IEPC blank form on the overhead projector and tell the students that they are going to engage in a strategy designed to encourage them to use their imaginations to create mental pictures. Tell them that making mental pictures before, during, and after reading will help them understand and remember what they read.

> **Step Three:** Use the transparency to point out and explain the four phases of IEPC, using language appropriate to their ability levels.

Prereading Stage

> **Step Four:** Tell the students that they are going to read (or hear) a selection. Begin with the imagine phase and ask the students to join you in closing their eyes and

imagining everything they can about the selection to be read. Their thoughts may be based on the cover of the book, a title, or a topic. Encourage the students to use sensory experiences by imagining feelings, taste, smell, sight, and surroundings.

Step Five: Share your thoughts and then ask the class if they have anything to add. Write the responses in the I column on the form.

Step Six: Model for the students how they can use their visual images and add details, anecdotes, prior experiences, sensory information, and so on. Jot this information in the E column.

Step Seven: Make at least one sample prediction, based on prior visual images and encourage the students to do the same. Write these responses in the P column.

Reading Stage

Step Eight: Have students read or listen to the selection with these predictions in mind.

Postreading Stage

Step Nine: After reading, return to the transparency and, using a different color marker, modify the original predictions to coordinate with the newly learned information.

Source: Based on Wood, K. D., & Endres, C. (2004/5). Motivating student interest with the Imagine, Elaborate, Predict and Confirm (IEPC) strategy. *The Reading Teacher, 58*(4), 346–357.

Imagine, Elaborate, Predict, and Confirm (IEPC) Sample Exercise

Student responses before and after reading *A Snake in the House,* **by Faith McNulty**

I	E	P	C
The snake is slimy, and it slithers and flicks its tongue. I feel nervous and scared. I see the snake moving quickly across the floor.	The snake's scales are slimy, and its dark cold eyes stare at me. The snake is crawling through the house, and I am afraid it will bite me. The snake slithers quickly across the floor as it searches for something to eat.	The snake and the cat will fight, and the snake will bite the cat in the neck. Someone will catch the snake and take it outside.	The snake searches the house for food and a way to escape. The cat tries to catch the snake, but the snake gets away. The snake crawls into a basket and the boy carries it outside. Finally, the boy grabs the snake and sets it free. The snake felt warm, dry, and alive. It has a powerful body. It crawls quickly through the grass toward its home.

Imagine, Elaborate, Predict, and Confirm (IEPC) Sample Exercise

Student responses before and after reading *Wolf*, by Becky Bloom

I	E	P	C
Close your eyes and imagine the scene, character, and events. What do you see, feel, hear, and smell? Share your thinking with a partner.	Elaborate, tell, describe, or give details of what you see in your mind.	Use these ideas to make some predictions and guesses about the passage to be read.	Read to confirm or change your predictions about the passage.
mean black howls growls brownish teeth scary nice	I see a big brownish-black wolf with his teeth showing. He is growling and licking his lips. He's hungry and pacing back and forth. I see a storybook wolf who ends up being nice to everyone.	I predict he will try to attack some little animals or people. Hunters will probably have to go after him. Maybe he'll get something to eat and calm down.	He looks like a wolf but he goes to school, wears glasses, and reads. He starts off being mean but the duck, pig, and cow ignore him since they are reading. He tries to scare the animals by howling and jumping at them. Only the chickens and rabbits run away. He goes to school and learns to read. He does calm down when he learns to read.

Imagine, Elaborate, Predict, and Confirm (IEPC) Form

I	E	P	C
Close your eyes and imagine the scene, character, and events. What do you see, feel, hear, and smell? Share your thinking with a partner.	Elaborate, tell, describe, or give details of what you see in your mind.	Use these ideas to make some predictions or guesses about the passages to be read.	Read to confirm or change your predictions about the passage.

Copyright © 2006 Allyn and Bacon, Pearson Education, Inc.

STRATEGY 21

Story Maps and Frames

Objective: To help focus students' writing in response to reading and to enhance comprehension

Rationale/Description: Story maps or frames provide a sequence of spaces for connecting key language elements to help students focus their writing. The purpose of story frames is threefold: (1) to provide a framework to guide students' understanding and responding, (2) to give a structured format to follow for engaging in a writing activity, and (3) to help students develop independent comprehension strategies.

Intended for: Elementary, intermediate, middle, and secondary students, particularly beginning readers and writers and students who need additional support

Procedures:

Modeling Stage (Whole Class)

Step One: Use the blank forms included here and display it on an overhead projector. Ask the students if they have ever had problems deciding what to write about when asked to summarize a selection. Explain to the students that this frame, like the frame of a new house, will allow them to fill the blanks with information from the selection just read.

Step Two: With the students following along, read the problem–solution frame aloud and explain that many stories they read have a problem that occurs that must be solved by one of the characters.

Step Three: Read a story aloud that follows the problem–solution theme and together with the class fill in the frame. It may be necessary for the teacher to think aloud a few examples to model the process.

Step Four: Have students volunteer to read the frame orally.

Guided Practice (Small Group, Pairs)

Step Five: Introduce a story that students may read silently, out loud in pairs, or a combination of both.

Step Six: After reading and discussing the story, have the students work in pairs (or groups) to produce one common frame.

Step Seven: Have students share their frames with others to determine how their composition sounds. Optional peer editing can be employed here.

Step Eight: Repeat the process using other frame formats as deemed necessary.

Independent Practice

Step Nine: After modeling and practicing various frames, blank frames can be made available in the reading corner.

Step Ten: Students can choose their own stories and complete the appropriate frame.

Step Eleven: Students may be asked to share and edit their frames with a partner before turning them in for credit.

Step Twelve: When deemed appropriate, allow students to write summaries first in pairs and then on their own without the aid of partners or a frame.

Source: Based on Fowler, G. (1982, November). Developing comprehension skills in primary students through the use of story frames. *The Reading Teacher, 36*(2).

Important Idea or Plot Frame—Sample Exercise

The Three Little Pigs

In this story, a problem begins when three pigs decide to build houses made of
three different things .

After that, a big, bad wolf comes along to eat them .

Next the wolf blows down the house made of straw and eats the pig who lives inside .

Then the wolf blows down the house made of sticks and eats the pig who lives there .

The problem is solved when the wolf tries to blow down the house made of bricks, but he
can't do it .

The story ends when the wolf dies from trying so hard to blow down the brick house .

Story Map Sample Exercise

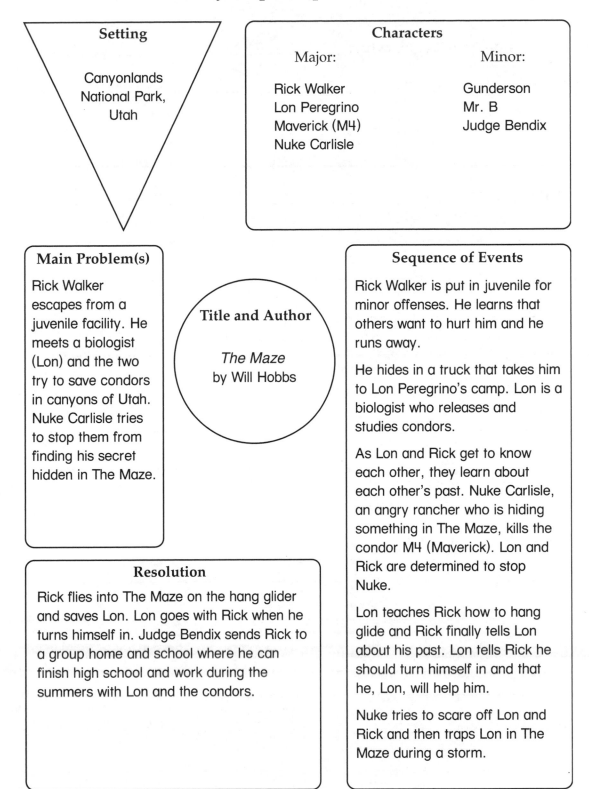

Setting

Canyonlands National Park, Utah

Characters

Major:

Rick Walker
Lon Peregrino
Maverick (M4)
Nuke Carlisle

Minor:

Gunderson
Mr. B
Judge Bendix

Main Problem(s)

Rick Walker escapes from a juvenile facility. He meets a biologist (Lon) and the two try to save condors in canyons of Utah. Nuke Carlisle tries to stop them from finding his secret hidden in The Maze.

Title and Author

The Maze
by Will Hobbs

Sequence of Events

Rick Walker is put in juvenile for minor offenses. He learns that others want to hurt him and he runs away.

He hides in a truck that takes him to Lon Peregrino's camp. Lon is a biologist who releases and studies condors.

As Lon and Rick get to know each other, they learn about each other's past. Nuke Carlisle, an angry rancher who is hiding something in The Maze, kills the condor M4 (Maverick). Lon and Rick are determined to stop Nuke.

Lon teaches Rick how to hang glide and Rick finally tells Lon about his past. Lon tells Rick he should turn himself in and that he, Lon, will help him.

Nuke tries to scare off Lon and Rick and then traps Lon in The Maze during a storm.

Resolution

Rick flies into The Maze on the hang glider and saves Lon. Lon goes with Rick when he turns himself in. Judge Bendix sends Rick to a group home and school where he can finish high school and work during the summers with Lon and the condors.

Important Idea or Plot Frame

In this story, a problem begins when _____

_____

_____

_____ .

After that, _____

_____ .

Next _____

_____

_____ .

Then _____

_____

_____

_____ .

The problem is solved when _____

_____

_____

_____ .

The story ends when _____

_____

_____

_____ .

Copyright © 2006 Allyn and Bacon, Pearson Education, Inc.

Story Map

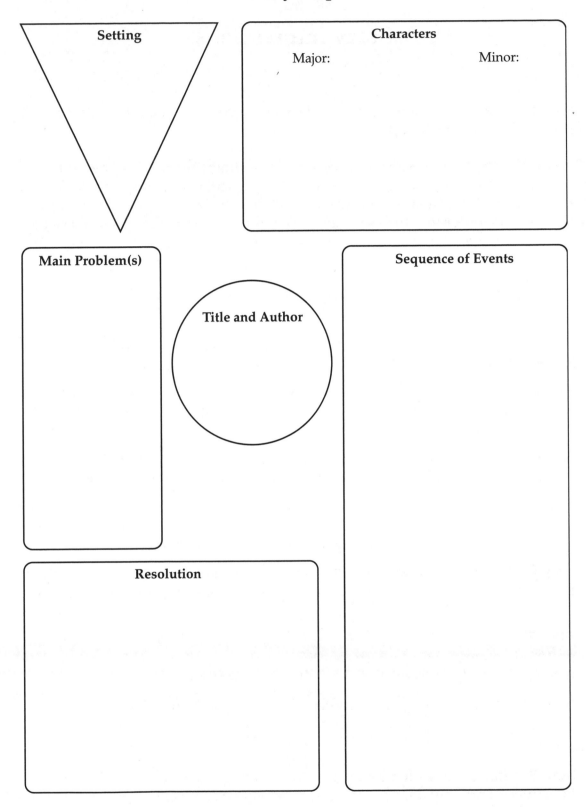

Setting

Characters

Major: Minor:

Main Problem(s)

Title and Author

Sequence of Events

Resolution

Copyright © 2006 Allyn and Bacon, Pearson Education, Inc.

STRATEGY 22

Story Impressions

Objective: To reinforce students' vocabulary knowledge, predictive abilities, comprehension, and writing performance

Rationale/Description: A story impression is a writing strategy designed for the prereading stage of the instructional lesson. It is particularly appropriate for narrative material because key phrases or words are pulled from a selection and presented in exactly the same order in which they appeared in the story. Students use these key terms to predict the story line before reading, thereby drawing on their pre-existing knowledge of how stories are structured.

Intended for: Elementary, intermediate, middle, and secondary students

Procedures:

Prereading Phase

> **Step One:** The teacher begins by selecting key phrases from the story or selection to be read, making certain that these phrases represent the action, theme, and main concepts of the story.

> **Step Two:** These phrases should be presented in the order in which they appear in the story. The blank form included here can be displayed on an overhead projector.

> **Step Three:** Read the phrases aloud to the students and have them repeat each phrase. Discuss and clarify any terms or concepts as necessary. Encourage the students to imagine and visualize the events and characters.

> **Step Four:** Tell the students that they are to use these key phrases to predict a possible story line. Remind them that the key phrases are presented in the correct order.

> **Step Five:** The prediction phase may be done as a whole class or students may be grouped heterogeneously with four to five members. The teacher can circulate to listen in, provide assistance, and monitor participation.

> **Step Six:** Ask the groups to volunteer their predicted story lines.

Reading Phase

> **Step Seven:** Have students read the story, paying attention to the key phrases introduced and how they contribute to the plot. Discuss and clarify the phrases with information from the story.

Postreading Phase

Step Eight (Optional): Have the students return to the key phrases and reconstruct another passage to coordinate with the actual events of the story. This may be done as a whole class or in groups, and may be done orally or in written form, depending on time constraints.

Source: Based on McGinley, W. J., & Denner, P. R. (1987). A prereading/writing activity. *Journal of Reading* *31*, 248–253.

Story Impressions Sample Exercise

Uncle Jed's Barbershop by Margaree King Mitchell

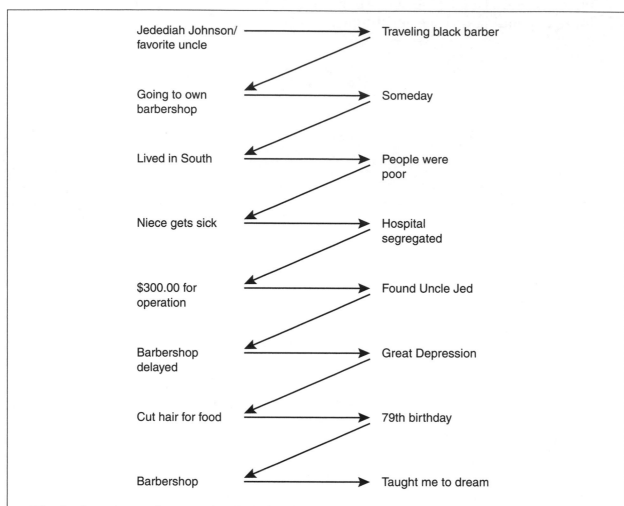

I had a favorite uncle named Jedediah Johnson. He was a traveling black barber and he loved to cut people's hair (Sara). He knew that someday he was going to have his own barbershop and then he would not have to travel from town to town cutting hair (Rodnico). We all lived in the South and we were all very poor. One day I got very sick and had to go to the hospital. The hospital was segregated and the doctor wouldn't see me (Queint). Finally the doctor saw me and he said it would cost $300 for the operation. Well we didn't have that kind of money because we were poor. We had to find Uncle Jed (Sara). Uncle Jed had to delay his barbershop because he didn't have any money either because it was the Great Depression. He gave me the money for the operation, but it left him broke (Rodnico). He was so poor after he gave me the money that he had to cut hair just to get food (Queint). Finally on his 79th birthday we bought him a barbershop for a present. Uncle Jed taught me to dream (Sara).

Source: Reprinted from Wood, K. D., & Nichols, W. D. (2000). Helping struggling learners read and write. In K. D. Wood & T. S. Dickinson (Eds.), *Promoting Literacy in Grades 4–9*. Boston: Allyn and Bacon. Reprinted by permission.

Story Impressions Form

Group members:_____

Part 1: Predict how the terms below might be used in the selection to be read.

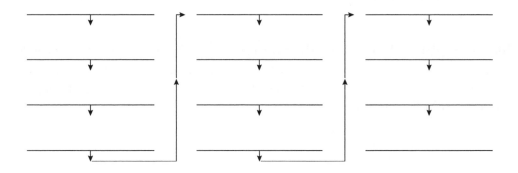

Part 2: Write your predicted passage in the space below.

Part 3: Read the selection and use the terms again in another passage.

Copyright © 2006 Allyn and Bacon, Pearson Education, Inc.

STRATEGY 23

Paired Comprehension and Retelling

Objective: To help students practice retelling with partners as a means of increasing comprehension

Rationale/Description: Retelling—the ability to put information in your own words—is a significant way to evaluate and reinforce understanding. Having students retell the contents of a narrative or expository passage to a partner is an excellent means of enhancing comprehension and recall.

Intended for: Elementary, middle, and secondary students, and students who need additional support

Procedures:

Modeling Stage

Step One: Decide on the material to be used to model, and then practice the act of retelling. It is often best to use material that is familiar and used in the classroom.

Step Two: Explain to the students that one of the best ways to help them remember what they read is to recite the content, using their own words as often as possible. Tell them that they are going to learn a strategy to help them know how to retell information.

Step Three: Display the retelling form on an overhead projector. Then, read aloud a brief passage to the class and put the information in your own words. (Concentrate on either narrative or expository material for the introductory and practice sessions, then introduce the others after sufficient practice is achieved.) Focus on the characters, setting, and events of the story for fiction or on the recall of the main idea and details for nonfiction. Model how to elaborate, imagine, and relate content to prior experiences.

Step Four: Ask the class to join you in evaluating the retelling, marking the responses on the transparency.

Guided Practice

Step Five: Have students open their books to a specified passage or hand out a passage for practice. Assign students to partners and have them softly read the passage together, read to one another, or read the selection silently.

Step Six: Encourage partners to add to and embellish each other's retellings with analogies, anecdotes, and questions about the topic.

Step Seven: As the partners work together to write their brief retellings in the space provided, monitor the students to evaluate and provide assistance as needed.

Independent Practice

Step Eight: Have students practice individually, putting information in their own words after reading both with and without the form.

Step Nine: Tell the class to apply the strategy of retelling, either mentally or in writing, when they read and study other subjects.

Source: Adapted from Koskinen, P. S., Gambrell, L. G., Kapinus, B., & Heathington, B. (1988). Retelling: A strategy for enhancing students' reading comprehension. *The Reading Teacher, 41*(9), 892–896.

Retelling Form

Name:_____ Partner: _____

I listened to _____ .

Choose one or more things your partner did well:

Fiction—My partner told about

____ The characters

____ The setting

____ The events in the story

____ The beginning

____ The ending

____ The problem

____ The resolution (how the problem was solved)

Nonfiction—My partner told about

____ The main ideas

____ The details

With the aid of your partner, retell the selection in your own words in the space below.

_____

_____

_____

_____

_____

_____

_____

_____

Copyright © 2006 Allyn and Bacon, Pearson Education, Inc.

STRATEGY 24

RAFT

Objective: To help students structure writing assignments, enabling them to learn more about content material as well as learning about writing for specific audiences

Rationale/Description: RAFT is a system to help students understand their roles as writers (R), the audience they will address (A), the varied formats for writing (F), and the expected topic (T). Almost all RAFT writing assignments are written from a viewpoint other than the student's, to another audience rather than to the teacher, and in a form different from the ordinary theme.

Intended for: Upper elementary and intermediate students and above

Procedures:

Explanation

Step One: Explain to the students how all writers have to consider various aspects before every writing assignment including role, audience, format, and topic. Tell them that they are going to structure their writing around these elements. (It is helpful to display these elements on chart paper or bulletin board for future reference.)

- **Role of the writer (R).** Who or what are you? (A scientist, a car, George Washington?)

- **Audience (A).** To whom is this written? (A friend, a police officer, a parent?)

- **Format (F).** What kind of form will it take? (A journal entry, a letter, a memo, a list, a poem, a song, an advertisement?)

- **Topic plus a strong verb (T).** (Persuade a company to hire you, demand for fair treatment as a slave, plead for a ride on a rocket ship.)

Step Two: Display a completed RAFT example (such as the one that follows) on the overhead and discuss the key elements as a class.

Modeling/Demonstration

Step Three: Then think aloud another sample RAFT exercise with the aid of the class. Brainstorm additional topic ideas and write down the suggestions listing roles, audiences, formats, and strong verbs associated with each topic.

Step Four: Assign students to pairs or small, heterogeneous groups of four or five and have them put their heads together to write about a chosen topic with one RAFT assignment between them.

Guided Practice

Step Five: Circulate among the groups to provide assistance as needed. Then have the groups share their completed assignments with the class.

Step Six: After students become more proficient in developing this style of writing, have them generate RAFT assignments of their own based on current topics studied in class.

Source: Based on Santa, C. M. (1988). *Content reading including study systems: Reading writing and studying across the curriculum.* Dubuque, IA: Kendall/Hunt.

RAFT Sample Exercise

Fourth-Grade Math (Division/Sharing)

R   **Math operation (division)**
A   **Classmates**
F   **Speech or letter**
T   **Convince audience that division has many important daily uses.**

Dear Students,

My name is Division, and I am a mathematical operation that can help you in many ways. Sadly, sometimes students seem afraid of me, or think that I am too confusing to be useful But if you give me a chance, you will see that I can save you valuable time, and maybe even help you keep your friends!

For example, imagine that you and your two best friends just ordered a pizza for lunch. The pizza is cut into 12 slices, and you are wondering how to decide how many slices of pizza you and you friends should eat. You want to be fair to everyone, but you aren't sure how many slices each of you should get. You could count out the slices one by one, but the pizza would be cold before you finished! So to solve your problem, you divide.

You have 12 slices of pizza, right? And two friends, plus you, equals three people to eat the pizza. If you divide 12 by three, the answer you get is four. So that's it: You and each of your friends is allowed to eat four slices of hot, delicious pizza! And you figured it out in no time at all!

So you see, division can be a very helpful tool. I can help you solve many problems: I could tell you how 5 dogs could share 17 dog treats, or how many 8-person soccer teams could be made of a class of 24 students. Just give me a try—division can be lots of fun, and as you can see, I can also be very useful!

Your friend,

Division

RAFT Form

Name:_____   Partners: _____

1. Tell the following about your chosen RAFT writing assignment:

    R: Role of the writer (Who or what are you?) _____

    _____

    A: Audience (To whom is this written? A friend, a police officer, a parent?) _____

    _____

    F: Format (What kind of form will it take? A journal entry, a letter, a memo, a list, a poem, a song, an advertisement?) _____

    _____

    T: Topic (Persuade a company to hire you, demand for fair treatment as a slave, plead for a ride on a rocket ship.) _____

    _____

2. Use the space below to compose your idea.

    _____

    _____

    _____

    _____

    _____

    _____

    _____

    _____

    _____

    _____

    _____

 Copyright © 2006 Allyn and Bacon, Pearson Education, Inc.